The Arsenal Yankee

by Daniel Karbassiyoon

The Arsenal Yankee

Published by Hamilton House

British Library Cataloguing in Publication Data
A catalogue record for this book is available from the British Library

ISBN: 978 1 86083 847 7

Hamilton House is an imprint of Hamilton House Mailings Ltd, Earlstrees Ct, Earlstrees Rd, Corby, Northants, NN17 4HH

Cover photos courtesy of Arsenal FC

"Do not worry if you have built your castles in the air. They are where they should be. Now put the foundations under them."

Henry David Thoreau

To my parents who have always believed in me and inspire me to do whatever my heart desires, and for my grandma, Nonna, who never stopped convincing me to become a writer since she read my first work in the seventh grade.

Table of Contents

Foreword by Arsène Wenger   1

Preface   3

1.   Not your average Boy Scout   5
2.   The beginning   8
3.   Training by myself   16
4.   Goals, goals, goals   20
5.   Ich spreche wenig Deutsch   26
6.   The return   30
7.   Elite Soccer Program   32
8.   The trial part 1   39
9.   The trial part 2   49
10.   Decisions, decisions   55
11.   What it means to be a Gunner   61
12.   Off the field   70
13.   Make or break   78
14.   The shot heard 'round the world   81
15.   The kids are alright   88
16.   The Theatre of Dreams   96
17.   From Gunner to Tractor Boy   103
18.   The release   118
19.   Welcome to Lancashire   121
20.   Back to square one   138
21.   Down but never out   144

Epilogue   160

Photos   161

Glossary   166

Acknowledgements   170

Foreword

I had Danny with us at Arsenal as a young professional. He had huge ability and played as a striker. He made it into the first team at Arsenal on a few occasions and we were always very impressed with his attitude and approach.

However, as we all know, to be successful in football, a player not only needs that huge ability, but they will also need some luck. With Danny, he didn't have that luck. He had a bad injury at a young age, which is always difficult. From then, he just couldn't play at that level anymore. But I know Danny always had a passion for the game and I really liked his fantastic attitude. He was a bright boy and he was completely dedicated to football.

After Danny stopped playing, our Chief Scout stayed in touch with him and told me that Danny had the desire to scout for us. I had no hesitation in giving the green light, as I thought Danny was absolutely ideal for us. He loved Arsenal, he was young and wanted to learn. He also lived in the United States, an area of great interest to us, so it was absolutely ideal.

The biggest problem of a scout is to find the good players, but as well to imagine and understand how the player will develop and good he could be. You have to see some strong points in a player and how they can be developed. You have to detect as well how much they want to improve, how intelligent they are and where they can improve. That is what scouting is about. And I know Danny gets this.

I believe Danny has a big advantage and is a huge asset as a scout, strangely due to the fact that he had frustrations in his playing career. Let me explain my thought process... A guy that has done it all, who has won the World Cup, the Champions League and has been 14 years in top hotels and then after his career you tell him: 'Look my friend, you must now take the train in second class, and go to clubs on a regular basis, watching and learning football in difficult conditions,' I'm not sure some people are ready for that. But the guy who has been frustrated in his career and has all the ingredients, intelligence and passion is often up for this challenge and will make a very big career in the game. For me, this is Danny Karbassiyoon.

Arsène Wenger

Preface

If you're looking to read a book about a world class superstar who is comfortably making millions of pounds, dollars, or Euros and has won a plethora of player of the year awards, league titles, and other fantastic achievements, then I suggest you set this book down and pick up a copy of David Beckham's book or Patrick Vieira's book. However, if you want to know what it's like for the 99% of the rest of the professionals in the world of football aspiring to be those few superstars, then may I recommend you carry on reading.

In the whole scheme of things, and from a footballing point of view, it's safe to say that my career as a professional football player wasn't a glorious one with numerous star-studded performances. Despite making headlines and history on more than one occasion, my professional career, which lasted roughly 3.5 years in England, was filled with enough highs and lows to make one hell of a roller coaster. Sure I discuss what it's like to play in jam-packed stadiums in arguably the most football-crazy country in the world, but nowhere in the book will you read about me lifting the Premiership trophy or winning FIFA World Player of the Year. This story isn't about winning trophies and a multitude of accolades, but more so about making big decisions, following your heart, and taking risks when the odds are heavily stacked against you.

When I moved to London at age 18 in 2003, I thought I knew everything I needed to know about the country I was moving to and about the sport I grew up playing; however, the truth was that I knew very little about the culture, lifestyle, and opportunity that awaited me. I was never given a manual on how to succeed as a footballer in England or how to go about my daily affairs there, and I highly doubt one even exists. Though I don't regret a single decision or second of my time in England, I do at times wish someone who had been through the experience first-hand had been able to sit down with me and give me a little heads up about what exactly I was about to dive head first into.

So many people in the United States and other parts of the world think that being a professional footballer means getting to play in front of crowds of 80,000 plus every weekend, while pay checks with more zeroes than are worth counting are deposited into your bank account on a weekly basis. Although that is true for a very small amount of players like Kaka, Fabregas, Messi, Henry, and other international superstars, the other 99% of the players of the world are enjoying a completely different experience and lifestyle. It's not our fault for not knowing any better, and the fact that the United States' culture still puts soccer behind American football, basketball, baseball, and hockey doesn't make things any easier.

I hope by the end of the story the reader is able to better understand the craze that is the English footballing culture. I hope readers are able to understand why going on loan from Arsenal Football Club to say Ipswich Town Football Club is a good career move and can open doors that previously never even existed. I hope people are able to understand just how much promotion means to a club and a player and just how devastating relegation is. I want current players and future professionals to understand just how much hard work, dedication, and even luck it takes to make it in one of the most cut-throat industries in the world. Most of all, however, I want people to understand that with all that hard work, dedication, and a bit of luck, anything is possible, and even the loftiest of dreams can come true.

1. Not your average Boy Scout

The noise of the crowd is deafening. Even from the comfort of my own seat, I can't seem to hear myself think. I've never seen so many people gather to watch a game of football, and it's truly something special. 110,000 fans in all. It's not just any game, and it's not just any stadium. I'm in the second tier of the Estadio Azteca in Mexico City watching Club America fight back from a one-goal deficit against Pachuca in the 2007 Mexican League final.

The venue is world-renowned and for good reason. From my seat, I can see where Pelé lifted the World Cup in 1970 and where Maradona scored his breath-taking solo effort run, arguably the best goal ever scored. I can also see where the more controversial "Hand of God" goal was scored by that same Argentinean genius. It isn't just a stadium. It's a place of worship.

Mayhem is all around me. The home fans are not happy that their team is losing, and for every minute that passes the tension multiplies twofold. Everywhere I look I see yellow and blue with the exception of one section dedicated to Pachuca's travelling supporters. Surrounding their fans are two rows of fully armed riot police with helmets and large shields. Whenever Pachuca's fans become overly excited and start cheering, I can see cups of liquid go sailing through the air into their section.

The environment is hostile inside the stadium, and I'm having a tough time deciding whether or not I feel completely safe where I am. The couple sitting next to me refuses to stop singing. "Vamos, vamos America, esta noche tenemos que ganar." Let's go America – tonight, we have to win. They do need the win, and the huge majority of the fans in the stadium expect them to win. Every time the man to my left opens his mouth to sing, I can feel his warm saliva smack against the side of my neck.

Almost everyone seems to be wearing the same shirt: a yellow t-shirt with the phrase, "Mi sangre es amarilla pero mi corazon es Blanco," scrawled on the back with a picture of Club America's biggest star, Cuauhtémoc Blanco, plastered on the front. An incredible symbol of loyalty to arguably one of CA's biggest ever players: "My blood is yellow but my heart is Blanco (white)." Many will never get to see him in America's shirt ever again. He's already announced that he will be joining Major League Soccer after the away leg of the final, and for everyone his final game in the Azteca as an America player is too much to take.

With fifteen minutes left, Pachuca double their lead. Heartbreak for America and their fans. The crowd shows resilience and finds a way to continue to have faith in their team. The noise in the stadium seems to get increasingly louder. I look behind me and see a large fence with barbed wire wrapped around its highest point. Children, men, and women are all holding on to the fence and singing their hearts out. Behind the goal

America is attacking, multiple flares are lit creating a thick cloud of smoke over the pitch and a stench that makes me wince.

There are five minutes left in the game, and America seem to be given a lifeline in the form of a penalty kick. There's no question over who will take the penalty. Blanco steps up and coolly slots the free kick to his left. I'd wanted the home team to score the entire game just so I could see what would happen. Pandemonium. Absolute pandemonium. The fans behind the goal rush the fences separating them from the pitch. Riot police hold them off with shields and several fights break out. More flares are lit. Cups of beer are thrown everywhere, and I can feel the occasional splash of what I hope is beer hitting my jacket.

I feel something a lot harder hit my back and see a coin fall to the ground next to my feet. Two Pachuca fans are seated near me, and the enclosed fans above me are now throwing more than just cups of beer at them. Shortly after, the two fans pull their jackets over their heads and are escorted out of their seats by stewards.

When the final whistle is blown, the scoreboard reads 2-1 to Pachuca. My first Azteca experience is partially over. I still have to walk out of the stadium into one of Mexico City's less favourable neighbourhoods and try to find my driver who promised he'd be waiting for me. The thought of 110,000 people in the streets in an area I am in no way familiar with intimidates me. I decide to ride out the initial wave and remain seated.

Everywhere around me I see little kids and grown men crying. Never mind the result, these people will never get to see Blanco in their fabled kit anymore. Some, through their tears, continue to sing. Football. What a sport, I think. The passion, the joy, the heartache, the players, and the fans. I can distinctly remember what it was like being on a field in front of thousands of fans. I miss it dearly. I'm no longer a player, though, and on this specific day in Mexico, I can't really be considered a fan of either team. Technically speaking, I'm at work.

My allegiance lies with a club far from the craziness that surrounds me. The colours I respond to aren't yellow or blue, but red and white. My team's crest is simple but powerful: A cannon with the word "Arsenal" above it. I'm a Gunner and have been for quite some time.

How then did I come to be seated in one of the world's most famous stadiums in one of the world's most dangerous cities? How was I lucky enough to be able to say that on that given day, my office was the Estadio Azteca and my day's work included the culmination of the Mexican League? Most bizarrely, how the hell was I representing Arsenal Football Club from London, England in Mexico City as a boy from Suburbia, USA? I laugh at the thought.

I have to get out of here, I think. I've got work to do and never in my life have I achieved anything by just sitting around. I take one last look at the stadium and consider myself lucky. Football is my life and my job. I can only hope that I'm lucky enough to find my driver when I leave the relative safety of my seat.

2. The beginning

I scored my first goal in travel soccer almost six months after joining the team at age eight. I was playing up a year and was intimidated by the bigger kids. I wasn't exactly shy as a kid, but I always found it difficult to adjust to new situations where I didn't know the players and coaches. The goal wasn't really an act of brilliance or anything worthy of headline news, but it was my first goal.

My team was playing in an indoor tournament at the Carter Athletic Center in Roanoke, Virginia. Because it was a five-a-side tournament, we'd been split up into two teams, and I'd somehow managed to make the group that looked more likely to win. When the ball dropped to me in front of the crowded goal, I had several options. I could hear my teammates screaming for the ball, and I could *hear* my teammates' parents screaming for me to pass the ball. I ignored everyone and decided to shoot. The ball sailed past all the defenders and the outstretched goalie before hitting the back of the net.

The moment that had presented itself to me was perfect. I was still trying to win the respect of my teammates and coach but hadn't really done enough in my time as a Roanoke Star to warrant it. Something changed the moment I took the shot. My teammates knew they could count on me now. My coach knew I wasn't just going to be a player that filled a position. They all ran to me and high-fived me and rubbed my head. What a feeling. I enjoyed it and knew my parents enjoyed it as much as I did. I looked up to the track that circled the court we were playing on and saw them clapping, their smiles bigger than mine.

Even though I was eight years old, I felt like the king of the world. I enjoyed the feeling of success for all it was worth, and that feeling had no intention of leaving. I was young, but I had belief in myself. I trusted that I could do anything even if it seemed impossible. The goal didn't mean much in the whole scheme of things. At that age, my team always seemed to win and win big. It didn't get us to the next round or knock off our most feared opponent. It did, however, make me realise that I could have whatever I wanted as long as I was prepared to work for it.

When I look back at my childhood and everything that helped define it, I don't think I would have changed a thing. I was born on August 10th, 1984 in a relatively small city called Roanoke, which is located in one of Southwest Virginia's beautiful, green, tree-rich valleys. With a population of just over 200,000, Roanoke could hardly be labelled a metropolis, but it had everything my family and I needed in order to be happy and safe. My father, a determined and strong-willed Iranian from Abadan, and my mother, an easy-going Italian from Naples, were by no means rich, but they gave my brother and me more in terms of support and love than money could ever provide.

It was almost as if it was meant to be. The blood of a Neapolitan mixed with the blood of an Iranian was sure to result in a football-crazy kid that would eat, breath, and sleep the sport. Everybody always joked that I was born into it – that it was almost impossible for me not to have taken the football route considering my ethnic background. Don't get me wrong, it certainly helped, but just because someone is from a country that is known for its football ability doesn't mean they are going to be the next Pelé. My mom, for example, cared about three teams during my childhood: my team, my brother's team, and whatever team Italy put out in the European Championships and World Cup. She claims and claimed to 'support' Napoli while I was a kid, but I think it was just her way of getting me to ask her questions about her place of birth. I didn't mind. As I grew older and became wiser, I began to realise that my mom didn't know as much about football as I had once thought. I still joke with her that she's definitely Napoli's biggest fan. Regardless of her (in)ability on a football field and lacklustre support for Napoli, I still love her to death and know she'll always be my biggest fan.

My dad fell on the complete opposite side of the spectrum. He also had the chance to grow up in a country that was utterly nuts about football, but, unlike my mom, he took full advantage of it. He always stressed to me how important it was to get out and practise on my own. Inspiration would come in the form of stories from his youth that described him playing in the streets with all his friends. They didn't have boots or an official match ball, but they had each other, and that's how they had fun and improved. I envied that about my dad. No one in my neighbourhood took soccer as seriously as I did growing up, so walking out of my front door with a ball basically meant I'd be on my own.

Kami (my brother, Cyrus, and I have always called our parents by their first names) always made me laugh whenever he'd watch a game on television. "Who do you want to win," I'd ask. "Whichever team plays the best," he'd respond. Every single time. The only team my dad ever really supported was the Iranian National Team, and even when they played, just like every other Iranian I know, he would complain that the team needed to change and that something was missing.

My parents were just what my brother and I needed as kids growing up. Even though my dad was more of the enforcer, he still had a soft side that would come out every day, which led me to believe he was the coolest and funniest man on the planet. If my brother and I ever got out of line, my dad would simply ask in Farsi, "Kotak mekhai," which translates to, "Do you want a spank?" It was a simple question. Neither of us ever really wanted to be *kotak*'d, so he'd resume order between us with little effort. Other times he'd grab the pair of us and start tickling us so much that I'd end up in tears from all the laughter. Right from the beginning I knew I could count on my dad.

My mom was everything you imagine an Italian woman to be with two young children. If anyone messed with either Cyrus or me they'd have to deal with my mom, no questions asked. She fully understood the fact that being from an ethnically diverse household that spoke three languages fluently might be a hard concept to grasp in the South. If anyone ever said anything to me regarding my background or the languages that I spoke, she'd be right there to sort the situation. Never has a woman been so well equipped to run a household. When I was a kid she'd tuck me into bed and sing Italian lullabies till I was peacefully asleep. She learned how to cook Iranian cuisine to please my dad and his family, and her Italian cooking is the best I've ever had. The house was always spotless. Her jokes make me laugh simply because she laughs before the punch line, and her smile is contagious. I was and still am just so lucky to have my parents in my corner.

Cyrus played the role of big brother effortlessly. He was born two years before I was and actually asked my parents if they could throw me away the day I was born. Brotherly love. I've always thought that in order to make it as an athlete in this world you need an older brother. Not necessarily one in your family, but a friend who is older than you and can show you the ropes and put you in your place whenever you get out of line. Cyrus did just that. He picked on me, just like every older brother does, but it toughened me up.

Both of us had a lot of friends growing up, but we spent a lot of our time together as well - playing soccer, playing video games, beating each other up, and having fun. He once convinced me to play a game where he would direct a punch towards my face and see how close he could get without actually hitting me. With hindsight I'm not sure how I could have come out of that game as the winner. One misjudged punch and a bloody nose later, he told me to tell our parents that I had fallen down the steps and hurt myself. Cyrus taught me how to be tough in a way that no one else could teach me. I was used to him picking on me, but by no means was I okay with anyone else picking on me.

My mom would take my brother and me to watch my dad play in his adult league soccer games every weekend during the summer, and I'll never forget watching my dad wreak havoc on the opposition. He'd run up and down the field, feint one way, dribble another way, play the ball through a defender's legs, and ultimately score goals. At half-time I'd sprint across the field as fast as my short stubby legs could take me and jump into his arms. He'd be dripping sweat and soaking wet, but I didn't mind a bit. To me, my dad was the best player in the world, and his team, the Orange Crush, was the best team in the world. The field they played on was at a local Veteran's hospital and left a lot to be desired. The goals were old, the pitch was rock hard, and the nets were hanging on to the rusted posts for dear life, but I didn't know any better and loved every single weekend that I got to see him play.

When we got home from his games I'd help him make *doogh*, a traditional Middle Eastern drink commonly found throughout Iran, and sit on the deck of our house and talk about the game. Looking back at that time of our lives, if there wasn't a large chilled glass full of doogh to be enjoyed after the game, then things just didn't feel right. The mosquitoes would eventually drive us crazy and force us back inside, which meant I'd have to wait seven more days to see my dad in action. It was my first taste of soccer, but a taste that left a lasting impression.

During quiet weeknights at home my dad, Cyrus, and I would pull out a tiny cotton-stuffed soccer ball and go at it. Because it was only the three of us, we had to play with uneven teams, and my brother and I would usually team up to take down our dad. We'd either use the back of a couch, a doorway, or a mini soccer goal as our intended targets, and the three of us would battle for hours on end. One summer my parents gave my brother and me a really small goal with a plastic target that hung from the crossbar that would ring a bell every time it was hit. The goal remained my favourite toy for years and was used nearly every night by the three of us. Whenever my dad scored he'd always smile and say, "Yes!" After years of stubbed toes, numerous broken decorations, and several ruined couches, our free-for-all games basically became a daily tradition. We soon named the gamed *Yes,* and no day would seem complete unless my brother and I asked our dad to join in on the fun.

North Roanoke's Recreation Club, or the NRRC, provided the first organised league I would ever play in, and as a 5-year-old the North Roanoke Rowdies became the first team I would ever be a part of. My dad was the coach because my brother was on the team, and I was basically handed the role of team mascot. I was given a uniform but never really played because I was two years younger than everyone, and there were already enough players on the team.

It wasn't until a year later that I was able to sign up to play in my own age group, and I soon became a part of the North Roanoke Vikings. My team was composed of a bunch of kids I didn't know, but I was lucky enough to have several of my friends as teammates as well. The majority of the kids couldn't care less about our games and hardly understood what the point of the sport was. Many were just happy getting orange wedges at half-time and picking their favourite canned soft drink from the team cooler after the game. The weekends were different for me, though. I came ready to play, and, although my shirt was green and not orange like my dad's, I took pride in pulling it over my head each week.

Our games were played at a place called the Occupational Center in north Roanoke, and the pitch was somehow even worse than the one my dad played on. It didn't take long for me to realise that getting the ball on my left foot felt much more comfortable than having it played to my right side. I also realised that I had no real desire to have anything to do with defending our goal and only wanted to be responsible for scoring goals. I was put up front as a striker right from the start and spent match days trying to emulate everything I saw my dad do in his games. I started scoring goals and enjoyed the thrill of it like nothing I'd experienced before in my short six-year life. Although I eventually grew out of it, my mother noticed that whenever I took a shot on goal, my fingers would always be crossed in hopes that my shot would end up in the net.

The NRRC and the Vikings served their purpose for several years, and in 1992, after I turned eight years old, my parents asked me if I would like to try out for the Roanoke Star, the area's top travel soccer club. My brother had already left the recreational league and joined the Roanoke Star, and I wanted nothing more than to follow in his footsteps. I had spent the previous year attending my brother's games and loved the competitiveness of travel soccer. My birthday fell right at the cut-off date for the age group, which meant I could wait a year and play in my actual age group or just go ahead and try my luck with the older boys for a year and then join my real age group's team the following season. I didn't want to wait for anything, though. I was ready to challenge myself and couldn't wait to be playing with better and older players.

After practising with the Under-9 age group for several weeks, I came home from school one day and found my mom sitting in the family room of our house. She told me I had a surprise waiting for me in my room, and I quickly dropped my book bag and broke into an all-out sprint towards my room. I had no idea what to expect, but the idea of a surprise was more than I could handle. When I opened the door to my bedroom, the greatest thing in the world was strewn across my bed. Next to a big navy blue soccer bag with a Roanoke Star patch resting on top of it lay two sets of kit, complete with shirts, shorts, and socks. I couldn't believe it. I frantically replaced the clothes I was wearing with the kit on the bed and felt king of the world. The white and blue shirts were better than any piece of clothing I owned, and I couldn't wait to wear them with reason in my first game with my new team. My career with the Roanoke Star had officially started, and I was going to make sure I did everything possible to stay in the club as long as I could.

I never really considered myself a perfectionist until my first day in high school when I realised that my handwriting resembled that of a typewriter. I remember hearing the phrase 'practice makes perfect' and taking it literally. If a teacher or coach of mine expected something a certain way, I'd do my best to deliver my work to their exact specifications. Even if it meant spending several hours on a school project I had no interest in, I'd be sure to complete everything as best as I could. I didn't necessarily do it to impress my teachers, but more to prove to myself that I could do whatever I wanted to do as long as I put my mind to it. My parents always provided me with so much love and support in everything I did, and it was almost hard not to believe that I could accomplish anything I set out to do.

Many people saw my approach to my daily problems as conceited and overdone. I honestly didn't know any other way to handle life, though. I've always set my goals high in everything I've done. Even my school work was just as important to me as my time on the pitch, and I made sure to tackle my classes with the same tenacity and discipline that was so common to my sports training. Just like soccer, school was just another challenge to me, and I wanted nothing more than to be the best in my class. I managed to get all A's on my report cards until one quarter a fourth grade teacher sent me home crying with a B. Never had I been so upset. I made sure to finish out the year with straight As and kept that streak going throughout both middle school and high school.

That was how my mind worked. My competitive edge never found time for a vacation, and I was both pleased and annoyed by it. I always craved being the best and didn't rest until I was the best.

When I was seven years old my parents decided it was time to look for a newer, bigger house. I was sad to be leaving the house I was so comfortable with, but happy to know I'd be getting my own room and would no longer have to share a space with Cyrus. The backyard was far smaller than the huge yard I was accustomed to at the old house, but my dad promised me that he was going to get several truckloads of dirt dumped so we had a bigger area to play in.

The house had been built on a small hill, and the majority of the brick that made up the underground basement was exposed in the back. What seemed to be so great about the back of the house, though, was the fact that I basically had a full-sized goal to work with. The gutter that ran down the left side of the house acted as a post, and the lowest piece of vinyl siding served as the perfect crossbar. I used a little imagination to create a second post, and just like that, I had a goal. Not only did I have the perfect target, but the builders seemed to strategically place the windows just for me. I *had* to hit the brick. If I missed the brick wall by kicking the ball too high, I'd either bang the vinyl siding or smack the garage window. If I hit the ball too wide to my left, I would smash the gutter or run the risk of hitting our neighbour's house. If I missed right, two basement windows would remind me that I needed to practise more. I had no idea at the time that this little plot of land would be where I would not only single-handedly win the World Cup, but also lead my team to Champions League, Premier League, and FA Cup glory – all in my imagination, of course.

Despite hanging a poster from World Cup '90 above my bed, I have no recollection of the tournament. I was only six years old when the Italians hosted the world's most famous tournament, and I couldn't manage to sit still in front of a television to watch ninety minutes of football. A lot changed in four years, though. When the United States played host to the Cup in 1994, I was ready and couldn't wait for the tournament to start. FIFA had chosen the United States to host the tournament in order to increase awareness of the sport because, at the time, soccer was still far behind basketball, baseball, football, and hockey.

I did two things between June 17th and July 17th 1994. I made sure to record every single game that was televised, and in between games I'd run outside with my ball and try to do everything I saw in those ninety-minute timespans. I made my parents buy a number of VHS tapes and spent the days leading up to the first game labelling them appropriately. No matter who played, I'd record the game and organise it in the appropriate group or round. I wasn't able to make it to a single game and couldn't believe that the guys I dreamed of becoming one day were scattered around my country. Guys like Romário, Roberto Baggio, Bergkamp, Bebeto, Maradona, and so many more made watching so pleasurable.

I was lucky enough to be able to cheer for two teams: the United States and Italy. Although the States were knocked out by Brazil in the first knockout stage, it gave all American soccer fans hope that soccer was finally growing in our country. It also led me to believe that my dreams of competing in a World Cup could become a reality. I'd seen Claudio Reyna play for the University of Virginia two years previously, and now he was playing against some of the world's best. Being American and playing in the World Cup was a possibility, and I was so excited about the thought of it. After watching Brazil sink the Italians in penalties in the final, I had roughly fifteen tapes with three games apiece on them. I had enough footage to watch for four years until France '98 came around and enough inspiration for a lifetime.

I loved watching football on television and always made it a point to watch games whenever they were televised. The professionals I saw on TV were there for a reason, and I did everything I could to learn from the games I watched. I'd always have a ball by my feet and would pause and rewind tapes in order to see how the players used their feet and bodies to get around their opponents. After finishing up in front of the screen, I'd run to my backyard and practise until I was comfortable with what I saw.

I treated the television as a teacher and learned so much from watching the games I recorded. I'd spend hours watching my favourite players and even began memorising the commentary whenever goals were scored. It excited me. I wanted those commentators to be saying my name in the future but knew that just watching football wouldn't improve my game. It certainly helped give me ideas and accelerate my creativity on the field, but I needed to practise what I saw.

My career with the Roanoke Star continued after my initial season in 1992, and my parents let me participate in the area's recreational basketball and baseball leagues as well. I was naturally attracted to basketball because of its speed and creative element. I also enjoyed it because I could practise by myself as much as I wanted, and I spent numerous hours at one of my neighbour's houses throwing up bricks and honing my freestyle street skills. The speed, or lack thereof, in the sport of baseball put me off the game entirely, and my career as a catcher, pitcher, first baseman, and centre fielder was very short-lived. I spent several more years playing basketball and only stopped when I was cut from the middle school basketball team in the seventh grade. This all pushed me more and more towards soccer and the transition to my one sport ways. With a ball at my feet and a goal to attack, I felt at home on a soccer field and started focusing on the game that would eventually give me much more than I ever anticipated.

3. Training by myself

In the tenth grade, I finally decided to concentrate solely on soccer and 'retired' from every other sport I had played growing up. Soccer had become my passion, and I had every intention in the world of succeeding at it. My club team trained only twice a week, and I knew it wasn't going to be enough for me if I wanted to play at the next level. I began practising in my backyard every day of the week. Even if I were only able to get one hour in, I'd do my best to spend some time with the ball. If I had club team training at night, I'd spend 3.30pm to 5.00pm in my backyard on my own, and then hop in my car and drive to training to join up with my teammates for another hour and a half. When I returned from training, I'd eat dinner with my family, do my schoolwork, and go to sleep.

The backyard was my private sanctuary. My imagination would run wild, and every day's session would result in me winning another big game or scoring the greatest goal ever. I could be whoever I wanted to be and play for whomever I wanted to back there, and no one could stop me. I even mowed the grass in specific patterns to make our backyard look like the pitches I saw on television. If I went to see a college soccer game, I'd come back and dream of making the College Cup mine. If I watched a Champions League game on television, the stakes were raised, and my backyard would turn into one of Europe's finest venues. My imagination was endless, and I was always ready to improve. When David Beckham smashed his World Cup 2002 penalty against Argentina straight down the middle of the goal, I froze the tape at the last second and studied his technique. He hit the ball so sweetly that it travelled literally one inch above the grass without any spin until it hit the net. Even though I was left-footed, I didn't care. I grabbed my ball and made my way to the backyard. Within weeks of watching him in Japan, I was able to hit a penalty just like he did with my weaker right foot.

I practised, and practised hard. I worked on everything I was good at and everything I needed to improve. The brick wall made shooting and passing easy because the ball would come back to me. I even practised my celebrations. One of the most exciting parts of playing the game was getting the chance to celebrate after I scored. The windows on the right side of my 'goal' reflected light perfectly on sunny days and were perfect for practising the wide array of celebrations I had learned from pros or come up with by myself. Unfortunately, when I scored my first professional goal, all the hours I had spent working on the perfect celebration weren't put to good use. After seeing the ball sail into the back of the net, a look of sheer joy took over my face and stopped me doing anything that was remotely noteworthy.

Scoring goals came naturally to me, but it didn't mean that I didn't have to work on my game in front of the goal. I wanted to be as deadly and composed as the Brazilians in front of goal. I didn't want to be the guy that just shot the ball for the heck of it and hoped for the best. Learning how to hit the ball accurately and under control meant I would be in total control of the ball. If I controlled the ball, I could control the game. I spray-painted small brown X's in the bottom corners of my makeshift brick goal and tried hitting them as many times in a row as I could. One, two, three, four, CRACK! The sound of the ball crushing the aluminium gutter, and the reaction on my parents' faces when they found out were awful, but didn't stop me. My dad tried reshaping the gutter so many times and eventually gave in and removed the bottom half of it.

To my parent's dismay, I treated the last piece of vinyl siding as a crossbar and challenged myself to hit it as I did the small brown X's. If I missed low, the ball would rebound off the brick wall and usually come back to me. If I missed high, however, the ball would crash against the vinyl and shake the whole house. Whenever I did clear the goal, I would cringe apologetically, wait to hear a window or the deck door open, and then proceed to get yelled at by my parents. Not only did I begin cracking and destroying the back of the house, but I even closed the vent that led to the dryer on several occasions. I'd usually forget to pry it back open and faced my mom's wrath when she attempted drying our clean clothes to no avail.

Even though I treated the back of the house as a goal for over ten years, I only ever broke one window. After dribbling through a series of cones near the fence, I unleashed a rocket that smacked directly into the middle of one of the windows to the right of the wall. The resulting popping and crashing noises confirmed the inevitable. What a strike, though. When I called my parents to explain that one of the basement windows was resting calmly in one million pieces on the basement floor, they laughed and said they'd been expecting that phone call for years. The fact that I hadn't managed to break a window until my senior year in high school was nothing short of a miracle.

Since we moved my dad had dumped several tons of dirt and grown grass to extend my playing area, but the nature of the backyard still made hitting the target very appealing. We had had a wooden fence installed to prevent the ball rolling down the steep incline into the small but densely wooded valley behind our house, but the fence wasn't able to stop everything that was thrown at it. It was simple: if I hit the bricks, the ball would most likely come back to me or be low enough to hit the fence; if I missed high or wide, the ball would most likely rebound wildly and go sailing into the woods. Seeing the ball bounce over the fence was the most annoying thing ever. It usually meant I'd have to spend the next five or ten minutes in the woods accompanied by snakes, ticks, poison ivy, and a bunch of other wildlife that I cared not to encounter. I lost a good amount of balls in the woods and can sometimes still see some from our deck when the weather gets colder and the trees lose all their leaves.

No matter what time of the year it was, what the weather was like, or what I had to do, I always made it a point to get the ball out for an hour or two every single day. I loved practising in the rain even though it completely ruined the grass and made the yard look like a mud pit. I laid cones down across our backyard and dribbled through them repeatedly. Left foot first all the way through, then right foot. I'd then switch and alternate between my two feet. When I was comfortable with the basics, I started dragging the ball with the bottom of my feet and using the outside of my feet. As I got better and better, I'd increase my pace and try to go as fast as I could. I wanted it to be natural for me on the weekends when I faced real opponents, and I did it so much that I didn't even have to think about it.

The only type of precipitation that prevented me from practising in the backyard was snowfall. The ground would freeze and make it impossible to do anything, and I'd be forced to work out in the garage. The brick from the chimney was exposed in the garage and acted as a smaller version of my goal outside. The wall was the perfect partner and helped me work on my first touch. I'd hit the ball off the wall, let it bounce once, and do it again. I switched feet, alternated between the inside, outside, and tops of my feet, and challenged myself to break records I set. If my parents had parked their cars in the garage, I'd grab a tennis ball and try to juggle around the cars or dribble through cones in between them. The snow may have prevented me from playing outside, but it didn't prevent me from improving.

I was driven to get better. I didn't want people to say I was good at soccer. I wanted to be *great*. Thinking about my opponents motivated me to keep going. "What are they doing right now," I'd think. "Are they out here in the pouring rain trying to improve their side volley?" It really was nonstop. After losing to the Richmond Strikers in our State Cup's Final Four one year, my dad and I faced a three-and-a-half-hour drive back from Northern Virginia. As soon as we pulled into the driveway, I grabbed my boots and ran to the backyard to work on my shooting. We'd lost 2-1, and the only way I knew to cope with the loss was by smashing the ball against the bricks.

When school was out for the summer, I would spend the majority of my time at a sports complex in Roanoke called River's Edge. Even though Roanoke was a relatively small city, the Roanoke Star had produced some good players who represented the United States at various age groups. One of those players, John Hartman, was a year older than me and was idolised by many other young players in the region, including me, trying to make it big in the Roanoke Valley. John was involved with the national programme from the start, and people could always tell he was a special player. *The Roanoke Times* often wrote articles about his success, and he always seemed to be away with the regional or national team on a trip of some sort. He was invited to the fabled Adidas Elite Soccer Program on more than one occasion and was eventually recruited by the University of Virginia. I always asked John about his trips and tried to learn as much as I could from him. He was playing in the teams that I hoped to be a part of one day, and the simple thought of representing the entire United States excited me.

I loved practising on my own, but I knew that it could only take me so far. I needed to work on my intelligence, quick-thinking, and decision-making and was lucky to have a small group of friends that I could work with. Along with John and his brother Phil, guys like Evan Bearding, Michael Bear, Adam Peters, Brad Collins, and Donnie Smith all aspired to succeed in soccer. River's Edge was huge and made up of multiple soccer and baseball fields. It was a peaceful place for us to train: Mill Mountain towered above us, and the Roanoke River ran parallel to the pitches. The summers were humid and hot and tested our endurance. There were usually no nets in the goals, so we'd set up a small grid and play two touch games. The tight dimensions and small goals forced us to think quickly and be creative. No coaches told us when to pass or where to stand. We experienced the same problems we'd experience in a full game but had to sort them out ourselves. The games were fun, but we all wanted to win, and our competitive sides always came out. The humidity tested our detemination, but tubes of sunscreen and jugs of water kept us going for hours. Once everyone was exhausted, blistered, and dying of thirst, we'd arrange to meet again the following day and drive home.

4. Goals, goals, goals

The increased hours I started putting into my training regimen away from team practice soon began paying dividends. I found club soccer challenging but was constantly looking to push myself to the next level. After successful U13 and U14 years, I was selected to the league all-star team that would compete at the prestigious Dallas Cup in Texas. Teams from all over the world were in attendance, and it was the first time I was faced with playing foreign teams. Our group consisted of a Mexican team, a Colombian team, and another American team. The competition was tough, and we didn't even manage to make it out of our group. It was definitely a wake-up call for me. The tournament made me realise that if I wanted to make it in the world of football, I wasn't just going to be competing with kids from Virginia and the United States. There were kids from every corner of the world who shared my dream, and I was ultimately competing with all of them too. The 1999 Dallas Cup featured a number of unknown players at the time, including Wayne Rooney, Glen Johnson, Kieran Richardson, and Peter Crouch. It was daunting, but it motivated me to work harder.

The goals I laid out for myself were simple but powerful. I listed both my short-term and long-term goals on paper and looked at them daily. They ranged anywhere from 'juggle a tennis ball 100 times' to 'make the U17 World Cup team.' As I completed them, I'd scratch them out and add another goal to the list. My top priority as a teenager was to make a youth national team, and at the time it almost seemed impossible. The selection process was long and being chosen would mean I was regarded as one of the best eighteen players in all fifty states. The thought of that was tough to comprehend. I couldn't start to imagine what it would be like to wear the United States' shirt and represent my entire country. Regardless of the road to achieving my goal, though, I wanted to make it a reality.

The process of making the national team was a tough one. Every state was separated into multiple districts where try-outs would begin. Players selected to their district teams were invited to the state try-out where they competed with players from all over the state. From the roughly 125 players at the try-out, a thirty man pool was selected to represent the state of Virginia. Eighteen players were selected from the thirty over the course of the year and invited to compete at the regional try-out in New Shirt. There were four regions in the United States, and Virginia fell into Region 1, a strip of states that spanned as far south as Virginia and as far north as Maine. The best eighteen players from each state would battle for a week, and another pool of twenty-four players was chosen at the end of the camp. Making the regional pool was a big deal, but being selected to the top eighteen in the region meant you would get the chance to participate in the inter-regional event and play against the other three regional teams in the country. If you played well at the inter-regional, you'd most likely be invited into a national team camp and be considered part of the national pool. The year-long process would start with thousands and thousands of kids from every state and end with just eighteen players who could rightfully call themselves national team players.

I'd been involved with the Olympic Development Program since I was twelve years old but always struggled at the state level. I was always unable to make any sort of impact within my age group and struggled to get into the A team from the beginning. Practice was sporadic, and I was very lucky that my parents were willing to drive me three and a half hours to northern Virginia for my one-and-a-half- or two-hour practices. Unable to return the favour by doing well with the state team, I found little joy in the program and almost feared going to practice.

Getting relegated to the B team was the first bit of rejection I had faced in soccer, and I rarely found myself on the pitch even with the second string. My good friend Ben Nason and I would spend a majority of games juggling a ball on the side-line while contemplating the benefits of quitting. I was intimidated by the bigger players, felt extremely uncomfortable with the new faces each year, and really struggled to enjoy state practice and camps. It wasn't the coaches' fault, though. I needed to learn how to adapt to new situations and leave the comfort zone I was so used to in Roanoke. As soon as I did, I began playing the way I knew I could and was selected to the A team after two years of repeated let downs.

I was tired of hearing the same words from the various coaches I had dealt with in the ODP program. "You've got a lot of potential, Danny, you just aren't quite there right now." I didn't want to blame the coaches and tried my best not to, but I was the sort of player who needed to hear positive things from a coach if I was expected to perform at all. Call it high maintenance or call it whatever you want, but I needed to know I had the coach in my corner, and I maintained that mind-set throughout my entire career. Todd West, the head coach of American University and my state team coach at age fourteen, was the first state coach whom I knew was in my corner. He was unlike any other coach I'd had before. He was very passionate about every game we played in, but most importantly he believed in his team. The players didn't just want to do well for themselves; they wanted to do well to please him. As a coach, he'd cracked it. Getting your players to play for you isn't easy, but he knew just how to do it.

Coach West selected me as a first choice striker in all our domestic events as well as our one international trip. I was playing with a newfound freedom that I desperately needed. I wasn't afraid to take chances and began scoring more and more. I'd heard the coaches tell me about my so-called potential, but Coach West had actually helped bring that potential out of me. By no means was I the new Maradona, but I was playing the way I knew I could. Making the eighteen-man roster that travelled to Oslo, Norway in the summer of 1999 helped boost my confidence even more. I'd never been overseas on a football trip before, and I immediately fell in love with the football-mad culture that was so apparent in Oslo. The newspapers were filled with football headlines from all around Europe, and all the sports shops were jam-packed with replica shirts of all my favourite teams. It was refreshing to walk into a sports store and see the shirts of teams like Arsenal, Milan, and Barcelona instead of the Washington Redskins, the Boston Celtics, and the New York Yankees.

I started every game while I was in Norway and returned to the States confident about the rest of the summer. Getting back to Europe was a must, but my immediate future was planned around regional try-outs at Ryder University. The week-long event was absolutely miserable. Session after session in the fire-like heat meant sore muscles, blisters, and dehydration. The dorm rooms were small and hot enough to bake pastries in. I did my best to ignore the conditions we faced for the week and focused on making the regional team. I'd never been so confident going into a camp, but I knew that nothing was guaranteed. As long as I continued playing the way I had been with the state team, I'd be set. I'd already scratched 'make the state team' off my list and wanted nothing more than to do the same with 'make the regional team.'

The week was long and gruelling, and when the final whistle was blown to mark the end of the camp, I was relieved to have made it out alive. I'd played quite well throughout the week and scored several goals for my team. The state team staff was happy with my performance, and so was I. When the final list was posted, I expected to be on it. I looked at the piece of paper once, twice, and then one final time. There was no mention of 'Karbassiyoon' and tears filled my eyes. I was reunited with the feelings associated with failure and wanted no part of it. I blamed everything: the fields, the system, the coaches, and the weather. I blamed everything except myself. I couldn't change the fields, the weather, or the coaches, but I could change the way I played. I could improve, and I knew I would.

Getting over the disappointment of regional camp wasn't easy for me. I'd seen the best players in the region at the camp and knew for sure I could play better than them the next time I was given the chance. I did the best I could to take the positives from the week and focused on improving everything that I seemed to struggle with. My U15 season with the Roanoke Star was just starting, and I couldn't wait for the year ahead. Danny Beamer, the club's executive director, was named as our new coach, and we soon began our year-long preparation for the U15 age group's annual three-week trip to Europe. Coach Beamer reminded me of Coach West. He was loud and passionate when coaching and made us aware of his expectations from the beginning. He was strict with us, and I enjoyed it.

I was very excited to know I had another trip to Europe planned in the near future but still had my eyes set on repeating my state team success and breaking into the regional team's setup. In October of 1999, while playing at Virginia Beach's Columbus

Day tournament, my personal progress came to an abrupt halt. We faced the Braddock Road Nighthawks in the first game of the tournament and were up for the challenge. The Nighthawks were a tough team but we were more than capable of beating them. Early in the first half, a routine shooting situation presented itself to me. The only defender close enough to me to be a threat was to my right, but he was too far away to make a clean tackle as I dribbled the ball on my left. If he was going to tackle me, he'd definitely have to foul me. Just as I planted my right foot to shoot with my left, I saw him commit to the tackle. At least I'll get a foul if I don't score, I thought. I don't know where the ball went, though. It's almost as if the guy mistook my right knee for the ball. A shocking tackle to say the least. Completely on purpose and completely uncalled for.

I hit the ground and grabbed my knee in pain. I was used to getting tackled but was always able to bounce back up and continue playing. It hurt more than usual, but I had no reason to believe it was anything more than a contact injury. I finished the game and the tournament, and even participated in the following week's training. My knee wasn't too sore or swollen, but it felt different. Every step felt unstable and after a week of no improvement, Anna decided it was best to take me to see a doctor.

My visit to Roanoke's top orthopaedic facility wasn't a particularly stressful or dreadful one. I figured the doctor was going to tell me I had a very bad bruise and would need to rest for a couple of weeks before I could get back on the field. He performed several tests, moving my knee one way and then the other. My ligaments looked good and I was happy to have avoided anything to do with my cruciate. After propping my leg up on the table and using his fingers to prod around my joint, though, I felt a sharp pain shoot up my leg. I wasn't a doctor but I was smart enough to know that the pain I experienced wasn't normal. He told me I had torn my medial meniscus and that surgery was required to fix it.

I was fifteen years old and full of anger. Why did I have to have surgery? I had plans that needed to be adhered to. I needed to be able to practise and get ready for my European trip. Most importantly, I needed to get ready for the regional team try-outs. If I missed the week at regionals, I'd have almost no chance of making the national team. The national team. My ultimate goal. They'd just started a two-year stint in residency at the IMG Academy in Bradenton, Florida, in preparation for the U17 World Cup, and I desperately wanted to be a part of it.

Because I was so young, the doctor decided to repair my meniscus instead of removing the torn piece. His use of tacks and sutures meant an extended period on the side-lines with hopes of saving my meniscus for the future. Being restricted to a brace and crutches was tough. I had three months away from any sort of physical activity, and I was doing my best to deal with it. I'd go out to support my team at games, and it drove me crazy. Instead of playing I'd spend my energy watching games that I had recorded from the '94 and '98 World Cups. I watched the games over and over and made a list of things I wanted to work on when I was able to run and play again. Regardless of how upset I was at being injured, I needed to face the fact that I couldn't change things. I needed to be positive for my recovery and take the time away from the game to recharge my batteries and prepare for my return.

I listened to the doctors and did everything they told me I needed to do in order to get back as quickly as I could. At the three-month mark I was back on the field and able to train. I'd taken my muscle strengthening as seriously as I could, but still felt a little uneasy about my knee. My right quadricep was visibly smaller than my left one, but I continued working on it to make it stronger. My club's trip to Europe was only four months away, and I wanted to be completely fit for it. I'd been looking forward to the trip my entire six years in the club, and there was no way I was going to sit any of it out because of an injury.

After a year filled with success, failure, and my first major injury, the summer of 2000 had finally arrived and with it came our trip to Europe. During our three-week trip, we visited Sweden and Denmark to play in the Gothia Cup and Dana Cup respectively. The tournaments were not only fun, but they also provided my team with the opportunity to play against good competition from all around the world. After we finished in Scandinavia, we took a bus to Essen, Germany, where we spent several days in a home stay with families from the local team. Everything in Europe was just as I had remembered it. The people were crazy about football, and I loved it. The results from both tournaments were published in the local newspapers, and everyone had football fever.

During the Dana Cup, Danny Beamer asked me what I thought about possibly moving to Europe for several months to play with a German team. He had several contacts in different parts of Germany that he could speak with, and the idea seemed very interesting to me. A player from the Roanoke Star had left the States to do the same thing a couple of years before, and hearing the benefits of playing with bigger, stronger, and better players made me seriously consider the move. If it were up to me I would have just gone to Germany and stayed there while my team came back to the States, but I had to talk it over with my parents.

Despite everything I had motivating me to push on and continue to improve as a player, my knee had other ideas. It hadn't bothered me too much in Europe, but it did swell at times after games. I assumed it was getting used to the grind again and thought very little of it. I visited my surgeon again at Roanoke Orthopaedic and explained to him what I was experiencing with my joint. After running the same tests he had before, he told me the surgery may have failed and that I needed to be opened up again in order to see what was going on. I felt as if everything was crumbling around me. All hopes of making the national team in time for the U17 World Championships and possibly going to Germany were thrown out the door, and the last thing I wanted to face again was another doctor with a scalpel. Needless to say, I felt as if someone had planned this specifically to halt any progress I was enjoying. Our trip to Europe forced me to miss regional try-outs, so that meant another year would have to pass before I would get a shot to try out for both the state, regional, and national teams. On top of that, I was facing another surgery and understandably had very little confidence left in doctors.

After speaking to several other doctors and therapists in the Roanoke area, a Dr Uribe in Miami, Florida, was recommended, and I arranged a trip to see him. Dr Uribe was in charge of the University of Miami athletic program as well as the Miami Dolphins. Pictures of Dan Marino and various other Miami Dolphins lined the walls of his office, so I knew I was in good hands. He conducted routine tests, asking about my surgical history, how the injury happened, and what pain I was experiencing at the time. He was surprised and appalled by my first surgical experience and stated that another surgery was needed. I had sort of expected the news, and in August of 2000 found myself strapped to an IV, waiting for the anaesthetist, and simply hoping for the best.

5. Ich spreche wenig Deutsch

I spent the beginning of my junior year in high school catching up on all the schoolwork I had missed while I was under the knife and in recovery mode in Miami. Dr Uribe had conducted a simple scope to clean up my meniscus, smoothing out any damage that had resulted from the first surgery. Within three months, I was running around and feeling just like I had before my first operation. The three month trip to Germany was in the process of being arranged, and depending on whether or not my knee was ready to go, I'd be spending all of March, April, and May of 2001 training with a German club and living with a German family just outside Hamburg. I made one last trip down to Miami to see Dr Uribe in February to confirm that my knee was in fact healed before booking my flights to Germany.

I had thought a lot about the possibility of going to Germany and the benefits seemed endless. I'd be training and playing with a club called Breitenfelder SV, whose U16 and U18 teams were part of the Regional Liga (2nd division) in the north of Germany. The first team was considered semi-professional and consistently found themselves middle of the table in the seventh tier of German football. I wasn't particularly worried about the first team, however, as I was 16 and hoping I'd be good enough to just get a game in the U18's. On top of the football, I would be receiving a cultural experience unparalleled to anything I could ever read in a textbook. The family who would be hosting me had three boys aged nine, fifteen, and eighteen, so I would have plenty of people to keep me busy during my down time.

Before agreeing to the trip, I was told my credits would not transfer from the German school. Danny Beamer, my parents, and I all agreed that repeating my entire eleventh grade year wouldn't be the worst thing in the world for me, as I'd missed a majority of the year through injury. I've never really supported kids being held back in school for sporting reasons, but I was young enough to be in the grade below mine anyway, and getting my junior year back might mean getting a better scholarship to a better college my senior year. With all the details taken care of, I was set for my adventure and flew to Hamburg with my mother the first week in March.

The family I was set to live with during my time abroad lived in a very small, 100-person town called Tramm about forty five minutes north of Hamburg. When we got off the plane, a frigid, Arctic-like cold welcomed us to the northern part of Germany. It was snowing heavily and continued snowing up until Easter Sunday. Kristof, aged fifteen, and Angela, his mother, greeted my mom and me at the airport, and after packing our suitcases into one of the smallest and most fuel-efficient cars I'd ever seen, we hopped on the Autobahn and zoomed down the highway towards my new home.

My mom made the trip with me to make sure everything was okay with my living conditions and to meet my new family. As soon as her week of reconnaissance was completed, she was taken back to the airport for her return flight home. It only took one week for me to get homesick, and not having anything familiar around me made things worse. The food was different, I couldn't understand anything that was said in the house, and I missed home greatly. To make matters even worse, one of my friends from home passed away within my first five days abroad after a long fight with cancer. I wasn't prepared to deal with everything and wished more than ever that I could be at home with my friends and family.

Although I would be repeating my junior year of high school back in the States, I had agreed to go to school with Kristof in order to keep busy during the day. The journey to school itself was a new experience for me. There were no big yellow school buses. Instead, I had to wake up around five am every morning and walk about half a mile in the freezing cold, snowy mess in order to get to the city bus stop in time for school, and I started wondering why the heck I had decided to come and live in the land of bratwurst and potatoes. Everything seemed wrong, and I remember almost asking my mom if I could just go home with her after the first week.

I fought through all my setbacks, however, and was happy to find solace in the main reason I had gone to Germany in the first place: football. Both the U16 and U18 teams were composed of big, hardworking, disciplined players who were very good technically and stronger than any boys I had competed against before. We trained on one massive pitch that was made of cinder, a coarser version of clay, and I found it very difficult to adjust. I knew the Germans had a reputation for being tough, but never did I think they would be this tough. The players treated the cinder as if it were a regular, soft, grass pitch, slide tackling opponents and going into tackles just as hard. Any football player knows how painful it is to block a shot with his thigh when the weather is below 30 degrees. The pain that accompanies the ball mark is borderline excruciating and can last an entire training session if not longer. The Germans seemed to take it to another level, blocking shots with their thighs while slide tackling across rocks. Needless to say, if you didn't have multiple "rock burns" from sliding in any given session, you probably weren't trying hard enough that day.

We trained three times a week, and on the off days I'd convince Henning, the oldest boy in the family, to come with me to Tramm's local football plot and cross balls to me while I worked on my finishing. On days when he wasn't up to practising, I'd go there on my own and work on the individual things I was so used to working on at home.

Going to school was an adventure in its own right simply because it was a German school with no Americans and basically no English. The only English I would hear was usually in English class two times a week. I took part in the maths class simply because

I wanted to stay sharp mentally. The rest of the time, however, I usually spent sitting at the back of the classroom next to Kristof, reading a book, drawing, or trying to read my *German for Beginners* book. The highlight of my day was the fifteen-minute break that allowed me to buy my favourite strawberry-flavoured rice pudding at the school's snack shop. The students were all very nice but hesitant and too shy to speak with me at times. To their displeasure, our history teacher decided to teach the unit on World War 2 in English so I could understand him. Although I had no desire to sit in a room full of Germans while either World War was discussed, it ended up being one of the most unique learning experiences I have ever enjoyed.

After the first week the three months seemed to pass much quicker than I had ever anticipated. Between practice and games, I was usually busy and found myself playing with both the U16 team and the U18s. I looked forward to training and made a couple of good friends on the team who shared my dreams of success at the highest level. Despite having lived in Germany for two weeks prior to my first game, the whole game day experience was still a massive culture shock. From the first blow of the whistle, I felt completely lost on the pitch. I couldn't communicate with anybody and failed to combine with the other striker.

Half-time came, which meant fifteen more minutes of gibberish in the locker room. I honestly couldn't understand a word. I didn't really care what the coach had to say, though. I had done a lot of running in the first half and was in desperate need of a drink. One of my teammates handed me a glass bottle of water that I put to my mouth and turned upside down. I took a huge swig from the bottle and nearly choked. I should have known. The Germans' affection for sparkling water had managed to find its way into the locker room. There was no way I could drink it. I felt as if I was dying of thirst and the only available form of refreshment was room temperature fizzy water.

My first forty-five minutes in blue had been a struggle and I was ready to make that change in the second half. I was still having trouble combining with the other striker and the team as a whole, but I decided to be more assertive on the ball and ended up scoring two goals in a 2-1 win. The goals gave me confidence and energy but, more importantly, they earned me the trust of my teammates and manager. My teammates were happy to see me at training and games and soon started inviting me to their houses on days we had off from training. I knew that as long as my football was going well, everything else would be okay.

Even though I was smaller than most of the boys, they still played me as a striker, and I ended up scoring twelve goals in the fourteen games I played in. The coaches worked on my movement, my passing, my finishing, my holding up of the ball, and everything in between. I was introduced to the local rivalry and soon started taking pride in pulling Breitenfelder's shirt over my head. After one game in particular a scout from Hamburg SV, who had originally come to watch another boy on our team, approached our coach and asked him about my availability. I'd become very comfortable with my life in Germany and was clearly expressing it in the way I played.

Before I headed home Otto, the U18 coach, pulled me aside and told me that if I increased my strength and continued working on everything that I was already pretty good at, then I would be able to make a very good career in German football. As a parting gift, and most unusually, the club gave me one of their Fila tracksuits.

My time in Germany was a big turning point for me and for things to come. Travelling to a foreign country where the language and culture were completely different was probably one of the hardest things I've ever had to do. I learned how to live away from home and deal with problems on my own. I was asked to speak German at the house and learned the basics quickly. The football had been so educational, and I really felt as if I was returning to the States much stronger, both physically and technically. I took back with me a first class experience and a unique insight into one of the world's most fascinating countries. Unfortunately, however, I lost much of the German I learned after returning home, remembering only one phrase that seemed to be the most important at the time: "Ich möchte ein Amerikaner, bitte", or "I want an American, please", which fittingly was my favourite type of cookie there.

6. The return

Following my return from Germany in May 2001, I joined up with the state team for a training camp at Virginia Tech in the first week of June. A lot of the players had heard that I had been abroad and were surprised to see how much physically stronger I now appeared. I was incredibly confident and knew I not only belonged in the state team, but also in the starting eleven. I was used to playing in super competitive matches against bigger and better competition, both mentally and physically. I used this edge as a huge advantage and was soon being praised for everything I was doing on the field. My teammates were shocked to see the massive improvement in my game, and I was happy to see the German trip was paying off.

I knew my work wasn't anywhere close to being done, though, and continued training on my own, with my friends, and with my team. I went back to the regional try-out with a point to prove and was selected to the twenty-four man pool that represented every state from Virginia to Maine. It was too late for selection for the U17 National Team, and although I was upset I didn't make the World Championship team, I put it behind me and set my sights on the future. I was not only selected for the 1984 birth year Region 1 team trip to Spain at the beginning of the summer, but I was also selected to the 1983 Region 1 team several weeks later for their trip to Germany. I had never even been a part of a regional pool prior to the summer of 2001 and was now getting called into older teams. Things were definitely rosy, and I was thrilled with every opportunity that presented itself to me.

I think my upbringing definitely played a major part in my being far more open-minded and adventurous than I would otherwise have been. I don't think there is any one thing in particular that I'd be able to credit with my awareness that there was more to the world than just the United States, but my parents made sure to retain a significant portion of their cultures in our household for my brother and I to be exposed to growing up. My parents didn't isolate us in those cultures during our childhood, either, and a large majority of my friends were "American" in the sense that their families had been in the States for several generations. The fact that one of my parents is from an extremely liberal country in Europe while the other is from a predominantly more conservative country in the Middle East helped educate me about the differences in our world even more than I realised at the time. So I knew that going to Germany was going to be different again, which made it easier. I didn't particularly know how it'd be different, but if Italians were different from Americans who were different from Iranians, then it was certainly easy to conclude that the Germans would have differences as well. I think the issue of playing abroad requires a certain degree of mental toughness that players who play at home may not have or were never required to develop. I'd learned how to deal with things differently by the time I was in Germany as a 16-year-old. At a time when the internet was charged by the minute in households, I couldn't just speak to my parents and friends whenever I wanted. I had to learn early on how to deal with things on my own and with the resources at my disposal.

As Thanksgiving approached in November I was selected for the regional team to take part in the annual inter-regional event in Cocoa Beach, Florida. This marked the first event that I'd be a part of where the best players from all over the country would be present, and once again I felt the same nervous tension take over that was so common when I first started ODP at age twelve. The games were so fast, and the national team players who joined up with their regional teams were a step above the rest. Two days into the camp, I received a phone call informing me that two more of my friends had tragically passed away after a horrible car accident that left my high school community emotionally crippled.

Once again, I was completely disconnected from everyone at home and found peace in the game that seemed to help me forget about everything in ninety-minute increments. Football was always my outlet, and that day I played my heart out in honour of my two lost friends and was rewarded by being picked to the list of All-Americans selected from the tournament.

College recruiting had started at that point, and my continued involvement in the state and regional teams started earning me recognition amongst college coaches nationally. Letters started coming in from schools like Wake Forest, The University of Virginia, Virginia Tech, The University of North Carolina, Duke, Stanford, and many others. My club team also took part in various college showcase tournaments, which helped the recruiting process. Whenever I had a free weekend from the Roanoke Stars, I would usually be invited to guest play with either the Richmond Strikers or CASL club teams, which were based out of Richmond, Virginia and Raleigh, North Carolina, respectively. Guest playing meant more games and more exposure to college coaches, and I was more than happy to meet up with the teams if it meant a higher possibility of getting a scholarship. Even though I had attracted the interest of many universities, I still hadn't been invited to the Adidas Elite Soccer Program and waited anxiously to hear from them.

7. Elite Soccer Program

My parents were the two most important teachers I ever had growing up. Both Cyrus and I learned a lot in our household, and we were lucky to have such great professors at the front of the class. Even when they weren't speaking, their actions spoke volumes, and I did my best to follow their lead. I learned that hard work was the only way to achieve anything. I learned that no matter what I achieved, I needed to remain humble.

My dad had a very unique way of getting me excited for games. If I was playing poorly, he'd just say, "What's your problem?" in Farsi. It enraged me. Before the thought of impressing college scouts and professional scouts ever entered my head, the only person I wanted to impress was my dad. I wanted to show him I'd learned from him. I wanted to show him that I could take what he'd taught me and make it better. If I was having a bad game, I knew I was having a bad game. I didn't need my dad to remind me. When he'd ask me that simple question, I'd switch gears and become a new player. After games he'd smile and ask, "Why do I always have to make you upset for you to play well?" I was a teenager, and a moody one at that, so I'd just ignore him.

As good as I thought I was, though, I still hadn't achieved all my goals. My dad knew I was inconsistent, and he also knew that he wouldn't be able to stand on the side-line for the rest of my life asking me what my problem was. I was seventeen years old and started developing a bit of an attitude. I didn't think I had to listen to everything my dad said and for some reason thought he didn't know what I was going through. When we were talking at the house one day, he told me that I had to remember one thing. "Here we go," I thought.

"No matter where you are or who you are with, always play as if someone is watching," he said.

His advice was basic, and whether or not I knew at the time, it went in one ear and decided not to come out the other. I sure am glad it didn't.

The Adidas Elite Soccer Program, simply known as *ESP*, was the biggest recruiting event of the year. Adidas invited 150 players who were meant to be the top high school players in the country. At the camp players were given all sorts of kit, including boots, running shoes, sandals, shorts, shirts, socks, and shin-guards. The most important aspect of the camp, however, was not the free kit, but the chance to perform in front of almost every respectable college soccer program in the country. Getting invited to the camp was a huge honour, and I'd been incredibly envious of John Hartman for getting invited multiple times while we were in high school. The camp was set to take place in July 2002 in Wilmington, North Carolina, and due to my recent stint of success I had somewhat expected to get invited.

Several months before the camp I received a letter from Adidas and hastily tore it open. To my dismay and utter disappointment, the letter informed me that I had been waitlisted and that my entrance to the camp would depend on others not being able to attend. I soon realised why I was very sceptical about expecting anything in soccer. I was absolutely heartbroken. I had literally dreamed of being invited to the camp, and my recent success suggested that I was definitely going to be involved in the Wilmington-based camp. I did the best I could to forget about it and continued training as much as I could with my friends and by myself. As the summer approached I agreed to guest play with CASL, a club team in North Carolina, and moved there to live with Robby Hoak, a good friend of mine who played for the team. The World Cup in South Korea and Japan was in full swing by that point, and because of the time difference Mrs Hoak would wake Robby and me up around 4 am every morning to watch our favourite players and teams battle it out in the Far East.

After roughly two weeks of travelling and playing with CASL, the number one ranked team in the country at the time, the team broke up so that some of their players could attend ESP. I headed back to Roanoke one week before ESP was set to kick off, having lost all hope of getting plucked off the waiting list. Two days before the camp started, however, as I was pounding my ball against the brick wall in my backyard, I heard the cordless phone ring in the grass. I always brought the phone outside with me just in case there was an emergency. I suppose that phone call could have been classified as an emergency, because when I heard the voice on the other end inform me that I had been removed from the waiting list and had to report to camp in 48 hours, I think I felt my heart skip a couple of beats. I laugh now when I think back to the conversation because the lady specifically asked me, "Will you be able to make it?" I wanted to respond with, "Are you freaking crazy?", but I confirmed my attendance in a casual manner and immediately called my dad, begging him to drive me to Wilmington that weekend. He didn't take much convincing, and a few days later we were making the five-hour trip down the coast.

Looking back at how far I had come in such a short period of time almost frightened me. Several years prior to the ESP invite, I could not even be found on a state team roster. Now, a month away from my eighteenth birthday, I was in the gear room at ESP, checking in and receiving my kit bag with everything in it. Registration was completed and each player was assigned to a certain coach. Each coach was assigned fifteen players and would be in charge of coaching and organising them for each of the training sessions and games throughout the week-long camp. Before heading out to the fields we were asked to attend a mandatory welcome meeting where the director of the camp introduced all the coaches and explained the itinerary for the week ahead. The credentials for each coach were very impressive; they included numerous former World Cup stars from England, Scotland, the USA, and Australia. On top of that we were told that Jürgen Klinsmann, Germany's former superstar striker, was in attendance and would be holding a session and talking to us throughout the week.

The last topic discussed was the all-star selection process and finally the Offensive and Defensive Golden Boot awards as well as the Golden Glove award. I specifically remember sitting in the auditorium at the University of North Carolina in Wilmington and thinking, "Man, some lucky kid is going to get to go home with that beautiful golden predator and I'd do anything to have that kid be me!" I thought about the odds of a kid who was waitlisted winning any sort of award, however, and realised I probably had little to no chance of even being mentioned in the same breath as the golden boot winner.

After the meeting we all broke off into our respective teams and met our coaches. Paul Mariner, a former Arsenal and Ipswich Town player, was put in charge of our team, and I was pretty excited to have such a successful player coach our team for the week. Coach Mariner's thick Lancashire accent frightened and amused us equally. His brown hair rested on his shoulders comfortably, and with his black-framed glasses he was able to pull off the rock star look with hardly any effort. We were handed our schedules and found ourselves on the fields for our first session almost immediately after the introductory meeting. The level of play was very good, and I could tell it was going to be an incredibly competitive week.

The week's schedule was filled with training sessions, games, and all-star games each night which were composed of the players whom the coaches thought had played the best during the regular games. Those players who were selected for the all-star games weren't required to take part in the training sessions in the morning to give them a bit of a breather. I scored two goals in our first game and was selected for the first all-star game, which was a great feeling because I was so nervous at the beginning of the camp. So many players at the camp had arrived with the "regional" or "national" team tag attached to them, and it was intimidating seeing all the national team players hanging out with one another. These thoughts always made me feel insecure about my own ability when in reality I just needed to ignore everything that didn't relate to my team and my performance.

By ignoring all the hype around everyone else and focusing on what I had to do for myself, I was able to play the way I knew I could play. On top of that, the players who came with all the expectations had much more to prove; after all, I was just the waitlisted kid who had nothing to lose and was brought in to make sure numbers were even. I was able to free myself of the shackles that I so often felt holding me back at bigger events where I was unfamiliar with the players, coaches, and surroundings.

I continued playing the way I had played in the first game throughout the week and was involved in every all-star game. Confidence pumped through my body, and I was absolutely fearless whenever I had the ball. If we played a team that had a defender that was known throughout the camp, I made it a point to end his reputation. I had this belief that no one could stop me, and it showed. I scored in every game I played in, including the all-star games, and constantly looked forward to the next game.

About three days into the camp Coach Mariner took me aside to speak with me. I was so lucky to have a man with his background coaching me. He had played as a striker during his professional days, and I knew I could learn so much from him. We talked about the camp, and then he asked me whether or not I thought kids in the United States would take the opportunity if it was presented to play overseas. I said that many kids *say* they would do anything to play in Europe, but whether or not they would actually take the opportunity if it presented itself was a completely different story. He also asked what nationality my parents were and seemed quite content when I told him my mother was Italian.

The week continued, and I was lucky enough to be chosen to take part in Jürgen Klinsmann's finishing session that was considered to be one of the highlights of the week. What a player he had been during his prime, and what an honour it was for us to have him running our session. I remember watching him embarrass defenders with the German National Team during the World Cups in '94 and '98. No one stood a chance when the ball was in the air and he was around. Jürgen's session was completely centred on finishing, and I loved it. Once training had ended Coach Mariner introduced me to Jürgen, and I spoke to him for a little bit regarding playing at the top level and what it was like. It was a great opportunity speaking to such a legend in the footballing world, and I'll never forget it.

About three quarters of the way through the camp Bob McNab, another former Arsenal player who was coaching at ESP, and Coach Mariner took me aside and asked what my ambitions were with football and if I'd ever considered skipping out on college to go pro straight out of high school. I told them I had never really thought about it because no such opportunities had ever been presented to me, but that I would probably consider anything as long as it made sense for me. The next thing they said was one of the most exciting things I'd ever heard or have heard to this day.

"Danny," they said, "we called Arsenal's chief scout and told him about you after the first couple of days of camp. He has been here throughout the week watching you. You should be expecting a phone call when you get home regarding a possible trial if you are up to it."

I couldn't believe what I had just heard and called my parents immediately after I returned to my room. To think that I would have missed the camp if it weren't for some player dropping out, and now I was possibly going to be invited to one of the biggest and most impressive clubs in the world. I still had a couple of days left in camp, however, and I knew I couldn't stop working hard simply because I was told a trial with Arsenal *might* happen.

Before I knew it the final day of camp arrived and with it came the final all-star game. Obviously everyone in the camp wanted to take part in the all-star games, but the final one was the biggest and most anticipated because of all the college coaches in attendance and the fact that one team played in France shirts while the other team wore Argentina shirts. All the players were brought into the auditorium, and the teams were announced for the week's final and most important game. I knew I'd be in one of the teams. I had done so well throughout the week and had been involved in every all-star game. It would have been almost cruel to leave me out.

I was named in the starting line-up for team France and thoroughly enjoyed playing with all the players who were meant to be the cream of the crop from the camp. I came out of the game with a goal as well as a dislocated finger, and I was relieved that such an intense, humid, tiring week had finally come to an end. I was also extremely eager to hear who had in fact won the Offensive and Defensive Golden Boot awards as well as the top goalkeeper award. My teammates were all telling me that I had done enough to win the Offensive Golden Boot, but we hadn't seen all the teams play throughout the week, and I didn't really want to get my hopes up.

The farewell meeting was held in the same auditorium as the welcome meeting and was incredibly packed. Several college coaches had decided to attend the meeting, and some of the parents of the players were also in the crowd. All the coaches and camp administrators were lined up on the stage, thanking both the players and their parents for such a fantastic week. None of the players were interested in the formalities, though. We all knew there were three awards that were going to be given out, and we all wanted to know who had won them. The first award, Defensive Golden Boot, was awarded to Patrick Phelan, a fantastic defender from Connecticut who resembled a brick house. The next award, the Golden Glove, was awarded to Aston Villa's current number one goalkeeper, Brad Guzan. In 2002 Brad was already a rock between the posts and fully deserved his trophy.

The final award was the Offensive Golden Boot. Rumours were circling around camp that the boot was going to either Ramon Nunez, a Honduran midfielder from Texas, or me. I was excited and happy just to be in the 'shortlist' made up by the players, and couldn't wait for the winner to be announced. Glen "Mooch" Myrenick, one of the United States Soccer Federation coaching legends, lifted the Boot off a table as my name was announced. Ecstasy. I had completely written myself off from being anywhere close to the Boot when I had first arrived in Wilmington, and there I was posing for pictures with the coaching staff and my prize from the gruelling week. I still couldn't comprehend everything that had taken place as I walked back up to my seat and was thinking something along the lines of "see, I told you I shouldn't have been on the waiting list" in a humorous manner.

ESP was such a great experience for me because I was able to compare myself to the other top players in the country in a great environment. I had gone in to the week with my main objective being to show the numerous college coaches in attendance what I could do. As the week unfolded and I started to enjoy a bit more success, I never let go of my initial goal and tried not to let any of the outside distractions get to my head. I started to see that achieving other goals was also possible, such as making the all-star games, and I started setting smaller daily goals for myself throughout the camp. This stopped me from getting too overwhelmed by everything at once, and it was satisfying completing the daily goals throughout the week while I chased the ultimate goal of getting a college scholarship.

Two or three days after camp ended, I was sitting at home with my family when the telephone rang. My mother picked up the phone and handed it to me after a short greeting. She whispered, "I think he's English", before handing me the phone and leaving me in the family room by myself.

"Hello?" I asked, with a puzzled tone.

The voice on the other end started, "Hello Danny, my name is Steve Rowley, and I'm the Chief Scout of Arsenal Football Club in London. I don't know if you've ever heard of us, but we are one of the biggest clubs in England."

I think I may have chuckled because of how funny his second statement was to me, but I tried to remain as calm as I could, sporting the biggest grin ever on my face. Of course I had heard of Arsenal. Heck, I could even name eleven players at Arsenal if I really needed to.

"Yes, I have heard of you guys," I said shyly.

He continued, "Good, I was in Wilmington last week and was impressed with the way you played as well as the way you carried yourself both on and off the pitch. I was wondering if you would be interested in coming to London for a two-week trial with a possibility to sign permanently."

I had kind of expected the call because of what Coach Mariner had told me, but nothing could have prepared me for any sort of invitation from the Chief Scout of Arsenal Football Club.

"Of course, I'd love to. When do you want me to come? Who will I train with?"

He continued, "We'd like you to come as soon as you can because we are in the middle of pre-season, and due to your age you'll be training with our reserve team."

My eyes opened wide. "The reserves? Not the youth team?"

"Your birthday makes you too old for U18's so you'll be mixed with our young professionals and some first team players. I know you'll do just fine, though. Why don't you take this upcoming week off and we can book your flights for the following week. A written invitation is already in the mail with the rest of the details."

The phone call ended, and I sat in my parents' rocking chair, holding the phone loosely, in total awe of the conversation that had just taken place. My mom and dad came back into the room and asked me who it was. I smiled, told them it was Arsenal's Chief Scout, and said I had two weeks at home before I'd be flying to London to chase my dream.

8. The trial part 1

When my dad and I landed at London's Heathrow airport the first week of August in 2002, it was the first time I had ever been to the United Kingdom. My dad had been to London before for work, and he spent the majority of the flight telling me what I could expect. My knowledge of England was limited to what almost every other American knows of the country. I knew they had a Queen and red double decker buses. I also knew they enjoyed drinking tea and spoke with funny accents. Most importantly, however, I knew they took their football seriously.

I didn't really know how to feel about the upcoming two weeks. I was nervous, excited, and scared, but most of all I was overjoyed at knowing I'd be walking through the front doors of one of the world's largest clubs the following day. Even though our flight arrived at night, Steve was there to meet my father and me at the airport's international arrivals hall. He'd been in Wilmington almost the entire week during ESP, but I didn't recognise him at all. If staying out of sight was vital for a scout, then he had definitely done his job.

We packed our bags into a strange car and were on the road several minutes later. Steve and my dad made conversation in the front of the car while I sat in the back seat staring out of the window like a five-year-old on his first road trip. He asked us questions about Roanoke and the level of players I was used to playing with. After getting a feel for my background, he handed me his phone and told me to call my mom to tell her I'd arrived safely. Steve made both my dad and me feel so comfortable even though we were thousands of miles away from everything we were used to. He discussed what a typical trial was like and explained to me exactly what I should expect during my two weeks in London. Hearing him say things like 'the reserves,' 'the training ground,' and 'the first team' all excited me. The next fourteen days were going to be fantastic.

After spending forty-five minutes in the car, we pulled into the driveway of our hotel. Sopwell House, the hotel used for the English National Team as well as many other national teams, was everything I expected when I thought of England. Located in St. Albans, a small town north of London where Arsenal's training ground is located, Sopwell House resembled a country club. Steve told me that the restaurant was already closed but to order whatever I wanted from the room service menu. He made sure that both my father and I were checked in before telling me what time I needed to be downstairs for pick up in the morning. After finding my way to my room and ordering a club sandwich from the late night menu, I lay sprawled out on my massive king size bed. I wasn't certain about a lot of things up to that point. I had no idea what the following day was going to be like, and I was both mentally and physically drained from the flight. I did know one thing, though. I knew I wouldn't leave England without a contract from Arsenal Football Club.

Despite being so tired from the day of travelling, I found it very difficult to fall asleep. So much was racing through my mind, and my body hadn't had enough time to adjust to the new time zone. Then, when my alarm went off at 7.45am my body clock thought it was 2.45am, and I found getting out of bed nearly impossible. I knew I had to get going, though, and after taking an ice cold shower to jolt some life into me, I grabbed my boots and took 'the lift' down to the restaurant for some breakfast with my dad.

On the way to our table, I made sure to scope out the buffet to see what was available. The tray of eggs didn't seem out of place, nor did the sausage and bacon. The mushrooms, tomatoes, and baked beans all looked like they belonged at a weekend barbecue, though. The tray labelled 'black pudding' looked like someone had left circular pieces of bread in the toaster for two or three days.

"What's that," I asked one of the waitresses while I pointed at the tray of 'burnt toast.'

"That's black pudding. It's basically dried blood," she responded.

"Hmm," I thought. "Maybe it's time I start looking for some Cheerios."

After putting together a light plate of fruit, cereal, and eggs, and getting over the fact that the pudding I had just been introduced to was not a delicious creamy dessert, I found my table and began asking my dad about English cuisine. Midway through the conversation, I spotted a familiar face in the restaurant. "Is that really…? No way," I thought. Seated in the opposite corner of the restaurant was Gilberto Silva, Arsenal's latest signing. The guy had just won the 2002 World Cup with Brazil. While I had been at ESP camp fighting for a college scholarship, he'd been commanding Brazil's midfield in South Korea and Japan. I couldn't believe it. I hadn't been too worried about the transfer window leading up to my trip to England and had no idea that he had even signed for Arsenal. The day had come at me way quicker than I was prepared to handle, and I didn't really come to terms with sharing breakfast with a World Cup winner until I saw him at the training ground an hour later.

After finishing breakfast, my dad and I headed to the hotel lobby where Steve had told us to wait for our ride to the training ground. I was anxious to get there so I could start training and work the long journey out of me. A few moments later, an older man wearing a suit and an Arsenal tie opened the lobby doors and made his way over to my dad and me. He introduced himself as Pat Boyle and explained that he'd be in charge of taking us to and from the training ground on a daily basis while we were in town. I liked Pat. As soon as I sat down in the car, he was asking questions and making me feel welcome. He kept assuring me I was going to do just fine, and I soon began to believe it.

I spent the majority of the short trip trying to get used to the passenger seat being on the left side of the car. The minivan we were in rumbled along several winding roads until Pat turned onto a narrow street with a gated entrance to one side. As the van approached the gates and cameras, Pat waved a key-card towards a sensor that granted us access. What awaited us inside the gates was awesome. I stared in awe at a uniquely shaped building dominated by large windows and a perfectly manicured landscape. The parking lot was filled with Range Rovers, Mercedes-Benz, BMWs, Ferraris, and Aston Martins. I felt like I was the guest of honour at a foreign car show.

Pat pulled the van right to the front of the lot and guided us to the main doors. To my left, a whitewashed wall with the words "Arsenal Football Club" emblazoned in red across it reminded me where I was. Next to the red sign was a large plaque listing all the trophies the club had won since it was founded. Ahead of me were two glass doors with the Arsenal crest on them. Pat pulled open one of the doors and welcomed me to the club. Inside, the building was modern and simple. Wooden floors ran from wall to wall, and framed prints from some of the club's biggest games in its recent history lined the interior. A frame-by-frame print of Dennis Bergkamp's famous goal against Newcastle United caught my attention and made me even more excited about the day ahead. The staff at the front desk all greeted me and asked me to take a seat while they called Steve.

My dad and I took our seats in reception and whispered quietly to each other in Farsi. We were both in awe of everything around us. I'd never really thought about a football team needing a reception, or a secretary, or security, but it all made sense. I only ever saw the players out on the pitch whenever their games were televised and didn't associate them with anything but the stadium and match day. Seeing all the behind-the-scenes activity that kept the club operating smoothly was beyond interesting.

After we had waited several minutes in reception Steve came round a corner and introduced my dad and me to Sean O'Conner, the man who was in charge of keeping the training ground in working order on a daily basis. Sean wanted to give us a quick tour of the building before I had to get ready for training just so I'd be comfortable during my two-week stay. After seeing what the club offered its players in terms of facilities, food, and medical treatment, I soon began realising why some of the best players in the world were so attracted to the North London team. The swimming pool's floor could be raised and lowered depending on the type of rehabilitation that was required. When players were exercising in the pool, underwater windows allowed the physios to watch and assess their every movement. Both a hot tub and steam room made minor aches and pains that much easier to get rid of.

Sean explained that several of the training pitches were heated to allow all weather training. Whenever it snowed, the grass would remain green and snow would accumulate around the edges of the pitch. Another pitch, specifically designed for players returning from injury, was composed of a special blend of sand and soil to reduce the strain from impact and pain-inducing exercises. The ground staff worked every day and left the pitches looking like acres and acres of plush green carpet. The chairs in the restaurant, located on the second floor, were designed to ensure players' backs wouldn't ache if they sat in them for extended periods of time. The Boss (as everyone calls Arsène Wenger) approved all the food prepared by Robert Fagg, simply known as 'Chef' throughout the club, before it hit the serving trays. Strategically placed security cameras monitored every move inside and outside the building. Everything was spotless, everything was in order, and everything was professional.

The last stop of the tour was the reserve team dressing room. White lockers and matching benches ran along the perimeter of the room. Neatly folded shorts, socks, towels, and training shirts lay peacefully on the benches in front of each locker. The *kit man,* or the person in charge of making sure all the training and match equipment was in order, entered the room and showed me to my locker. He finished organising the lockers before opening the double doors and disappearing from my sight. I sat down and smiled. Already so many exciting events had happened, and I hadn't even touched a ball. Resting next to me was a complete Arsenal training kit. I'd trained in professional shirts and shorts before, but only those that I'd bought at football shops or ordered from catalogues. This was different. I had earned the right to wear the team's crest, and it felt good knowing I was wearing it with a purpose.

Shortly after hanging my street clothes up in my locker, several of the youth and reserve team players began trickling into the dressing room. All sorts of English accents that I'd never heard before began echoing through the hallways and dressing areas. Most of the players just looked at me and kept chatting to their teammates, while others simply said, "Alright?" to me. I began getting more and more nervous and didn't like not knowing anybody. I didn't really expect the players to be warm towards a new face in *their* changing room, especially because more players meant more competition, and more competition made getting to the first team locker room that much harder.

David Wales, the youth and reserve team's head physio, soon turned up and introduced himself as 'Walesy' to me. Before I trained Walesy wanted to do a quick check up on me. I could tell he was sincere and enjoyed what he did. His soft-spoken manner helped me relax as he asked questions about my medical past. Both he and John Cooke, or 'Cookey' as everyone called him, let me know that they were available for any treatment I required during my stay.

About thirty minutes later I was standing in the reserve and youth team boot room, lacing up my Adidas Predators and staring at the huge number of boots hanging from the wall. Each player was assigned four pegs for two sets of boots. Once again, the room was kept incredibly tidy, and almost all the boots were free of mud and grass and polished clean. Even though the players were expected to keep their boots clean, the taps, brushes, and compressed air that made up the cleaning station right outside the doors of the boot room made maintenance easy. With my boots and kit on, I was ready to start the most important two weeks of my life.

Just as Steve had told me on the phone several weeks prior to my arrival in London, I was going to be training with the reserves. According to Ryan Garry, one of the few players who didn't seem to mind me being around, most of the reserves had travelled to Belgium that morning for a pre-season friendly. Only six reserves were left behind, and I'd be training with them. I couldn't really imagine training with so few players, and as we headed out the glass doors and started our jog to the pitches, I wondered what exactly we'd be doing.

Eddie Niedzwiecki, the reserve team manager at the time, had already set out numerous mannequins and cones, and roughly thirty Nike balls, the same balls used in the Premier League, were lined up next to the pitch. The pitch. Wow. Never in my life had I seen such a beautifully-maintained plot of land. The crazy thing? There were almost fifteen identical ones in the complex. If I had spent the rest of the day looking, I probably would have struggled to find one piece of grass longer than the others.

My first session was a technical one to say the least. So much emphasis was put on first touch, composure in tight spots, and the ability to play quickly and under control. The rest of the players were cruising through the different exercises as if it was second nature to them. The areas we played in were very small and forced everyone to think quickly and play even quicker. Everything we did embodied the style of play that is so attractive to watch when Arsenal's first team play. It wasn't rocket science and by no means was it revolutionary. The drills were basic but done with so much quality and concentration, and it was evident the boys I was playing with took pride in everything they did. It took a little time for me to adapt to the pace of the ball on the wet pitch, but as soon as I did I began to enjoy myself.

Even though I was just on trial, it was still pre-season, and I had to take part in all the fitness work. My stamina and endurance were both quite high because of the gruelling summer schedule I had completed in the States, and I was eager to show the staff that I was ready to run. The hot and humid weather that I was accustomed to on the East Coast was hell compared to the cool, damp London air. I didn't mind the fitness part at all. I'd always prided myself on being the fittest player on the pitch, and, even though I was working with professional athletes, I was prepared to prove to myself that I could still finish first. We finished the session with a series of strenuous sprints that left everyone gasping for air. I powered through the jet lag and finished near the top in every drill. After collecting all the gear, we made our way back inside to shower and get some lunch.

My dad had watched training from a distance, and as we ate lunch we discussed my first day. The restaurant and kitchen make up almost the entire second floor at the club, and it was pretty quiet because of the pre-season game in Belgium. Steve joined us, and asked me how it felt to have my first day under my belt. I was definitely happy to have a number of my questions answered: what the level of play was like, what the training ground was like, and what I could expect for the rest of the trial. I knew training would differ once the rest of the reserves returned for training the following day, but I was happy with my performance and left the club looking forward to a nap and the next several days.

The second day of my trial was especially interesting because a majority of the first team squad was in for training. Steve greeted me in reception again, but he wasn't by himself this time. Dressed in the staff's new training kit, Arsène Wenger approached me with an outstretched hand and warm smile.

"Danny, this is the Boss," Steve said, with his usual grin. "Boss, this is Danny, the American boy I was telling you about."

Mr Wenger asked me about my trip over and if I was enjoying my stay in London so far. It was a very short conversation, but the few words he did say made such a huge impact. I couldn't believe that I'd just shaken the hand of Arsène Wenger, one of the highest rated managers in the *world* of football. I had to start getting used to that and to stop comparing the entire world with the people I was meeting and the facilities I was enjoying at Arsenal.

As soon as Mr Wenger had exited reception, another familiar face approached the front doors. With a smooth strut and an aura of confidence that only comes with being the deadliest striker on the planet, Thierry Henry pushed open the glass doors and greeted everyone in reception. A quick 'hello' and handshake were directed my way before he exchanged his shoes for his flip-flops and quickly disappeared into the first team dressing room.

It was all happening too fast. I was still processing the fact that I had just met the Boss when France's goal-scoring super human had said hello to me. I didn't understand how anyone could get any work done around the training ground when some of the biggest names and faces in football were casually strolling through its corridors. Steve must have seen my exchange with Thierry, because he called me back to his office before I was able to escape to the dressing room.

"You don't need to be star struck anymore, Danny. At the end of the day, the job you want is the job they have. It's hard to compete with someone if you place them on a pedestal so high above you."

I understood what he meant but had never really thought about it that way.

He continued, "Obviously, you should use them as teachers and respect them and what they have accomplished, but you have to realise you will ultimately be competing with them."

His advice motivated me and excited me so much. I knew I wasn't up to the standard of Thierry Henry or any of the first teamers at that point, but I was in a position to be competing with them. Knowing I was in that position gave me even more drive and determination to succeed.

Training that second day was tougher than the first because my jet lag had started to kick in and I was already tired from the previous day's work. I met the rest of the reserve team and couldn't believe how diverse a group it was. The dressing room was filled with Irishmen, a Swede, an Icelander, two Brazilians, a Faroese, a Dane, one other American, and several Englishmen. The United Nations could have literally held a meeting in the reserve team dressing room and been fairly represented. The other American in the group was Frankie Simek, a boy from St. Louis who had been on the club's books since he was 12 after his family moved to England for his father's work. Frank and I would later become good friends, and we still keep in touch today.

There were about fifteen of us training that second day. The atmosphere of the group seemed quite positive because so many of the boys were friends. The majority of them were either English or Irish and had grown up with each other in the club. While we were stretching during the warm-up, Eddie announced to everyone who I was and how long I'd be in London. After hearing where I was from, Steve Sidwell, now with Stoke City as of 2016, shouted, "Hey Dude!" in a rather poor American accent from across the pitch. Everyone laughed, and I did my best to join in, although I wasn't really sure if I was being made fun of or not. Sidwell's joke marked the beginning of an onslaught of American jokes that I was so lucky to hear during my time in England. There was hardly ever any malice in the jokes, but it was almost as if some of the English kids wanted to remind me that I was a foreigner playing an English game.

The session was similar to the first day's work-out, but the increased numbers gave Eddie more options to work with. Technique was stressed and then stressed some more. Like the previous day, we spent the first twenty minutes playing four and five versus two. The possession theme progressed into a larger game of keep-away and finished with a game to goals. The football was absolutely fantastic in the game. I'd played against some very good players at ESP camp, but the pace and quality I was experiencing at Arsenal was far above anything I'd ever seen. The midfielders were the most creative I'd ever played with. The strikers were the sharpest I'd ever seen, and the defenders were the toughest I'd ever faced. I couldn't believe just how competitive it was. Everybody wanted to win and treated the game as if it was a proper match against a big rival. The tackling was hard but Eddie kept the game flowing, rarely calling a foul. I found getting comfortable with the pace of the match somewhat difficult in the beginning and saw very little of the ball. The defenders seemed to read every movement I made, and I quickly realised that I'd have to outsmart them off the ball if I was ever to get open enough to actually receive the ball. Even though it was a tough fifteen minutes, I was given the chance to see and experience first-hand exactly what the English game was like. If the standard was this good in the reserves, I couldn't begin to imagine what it was like in the first team.

After training, Steve asked if I would like to do some sightseeing, and I couldn't have been happier. My mind and body had been in overdrive since my arrival at Heathrow, and I was really looking forward to seeing a bit of the wonderfully historic city of London. Steve drove my dad and me around the city, pointing out monuments, famous buildings, museums, and other known landmarks. I sat in the backseat snapping pictures of just about every building that looked meaningful, while my dad and Steve spoke about the club, the Premier League, and England in general. I was content sitting in the back of the car. So much was going through my mind regarding professional contracts and college scholarships, and having the chance to get away from everything, even if it was for just a couple of hours, was very refreshing.

Once we were done seeing London's major attractions, Steve told us there was one stop left before the tour was finished. We'd left the hustle and bustle of the narrow, busy streets that defined London and were creeping along a quiet road that looked more residential than anything else. Plastered on one of the buildings was a sign that read "Avenell Road." I'd never heard of the street and wasn't exactly sure why Steve had stopped the car in front of a house on one side and a set of marble stairs on the other. When I stepped out of the car, I finally realised where I was.

Directly in front of me, at the top of the small set of stairs, two large black doors were firmly shut and locked. My eyes crept up the doors to a symbol that looked like an intertwined 'A' and 'C' that I had never seen before. Above the letters, a large cannon looked as if it was protecting the front doors. Directly above the cannon, the words 'Arsenal Stadium' were emblazoned in red across the white façade. The giant wall looked like a sea of white with red stripes. "Welcome to Highbury," Steve said.

The location of the stadium was incredible. Many of the houses that lined Avenell Road had Arsenal flags hanging on their outer walls. Stickers with current and past members of the squad filled windows. What seemed like a normal neighbourhood on a quiet weekday was actually the home of Arsenal Football club. No wonder the fans were so passionate in England. If I had been born twenty yards from one of the most famous football stadiums in the world, I think I would have been crazy about that team too.

Steve knocked on the black doors, and a small Irishmen who introduced himself as Paddy greeted us. He'd been in charge of maintaining Highbury for a long time, and

I could tell the stadium was his life. The doors opened, revealing what looked to me like a lobby and was known as the 'Marble Halls.' A massive red cannon had been incorporated into the sleek flooring and dominated the entrance. To my right, a large set of stairs wrapped around out of sight to the next floor. Directly in front of me, the bust of a man named Herbert Chapman, one of Arsenal's former managers, stared menacingly in my direction.

I followed Steve down a very small set of steps, took a sharp left and immediately knew where I was. The tunnel. As a kid, I'd been obsessed with football stadiums around the world. I wanted to know what it was like for a player to leave the comfort of the dressing room and walk out in front of thousands of screaming, passionate fans. There wasn't a single soul in the stadium that day, but I still felt shivers run down my spine. The tunnel was cramped and far from cosy. The floor was red and the walls that seemed to be closing in on me were made of brightly painted white brick. One final set of stairs led to the tunnel's exit, which opened up at the halfway line of the pitch.

The stadium was incredible. By no means was it incredible because of its technological advancements (as are the stadiums of today), but it was incredible because I could almost feel its rich history. The original stadium had been built in 1913, and it had since been renovated in the 30's and the 90's. I'd never been so close to the pitch, the tunnel, or the bench of any stadium, and I was now getting my own personal tour of Highbury. I stood at the halfway line, surrounded by the four stands that made up the stadium: the Clock End to my left, the North Bank to my right, the West Stand directly in front of me, and the East Stand behind me.

I couldn't get over what was happening. I hadn't paid to take a tour of the stadium. I'd earned the right to be shown it by the Chief Scout. The story wouldn't just end after I left the stadium that day. If I did well, I'd possibly get a contract. If I improved enough once I was at the club for good, I might actually get to play on the grass that I stared at in envy - the grass graced by Sol Campbell and Robert Pires every weekend.

Steve then took my dad and me back through the tunnel and led us toward the Clock End. From there, we made our way up to the luxury suites so I could see everything from a bird's eye view. The pitch was immaculate and looked like a fairway. Everything was set for the opening day of the Premiership. I'd taken about twenty pictures while I was driving around London and took nearly double that just in the stadium. It wasn't very hard to see what interested me more.

Once we finished up at the stadium, Steve brought my dad and me by the team shop and told me to take whatever I wanted. By no means was I going to go crazy, but I did pick out a couple of t-shirts, a scarf, and a stuffed animal for my girlfriend. We then made our way to an Indian restaurant, one of Steve's favourites, for a relaxing dinner to wrap up the eventful day. Steve spent a majority of the dinner asking me about my schooling and what plans I had in general for my future. At that point, I had a year left in high school and was keen to pursue a degree in architecture. My education was important to me, and Steve understood that completely. He mentioned that some players managed to take classes while still playing professionally, but football would always take precedent if there were ever a conflict.

I entertained the idea of playing football professionally and continuing my schooling. The reason I was going to go to college was to get an education. The reason I was going to play football in college was because I wanted eventually to go pro in the sport I loved. If I were lucky enough to be offered a contract by Arsenal and still manage to continue my education, why wouldn't moving to England be the right choice?

Our conversation shifted from schooling to my thoughts on the club and England so far. I didn't have any complaints. The training ground was by far the most incredible setup I'd ever trained in, and the actual training was the best I'd ever participated in. I didn't really mind England, either. It wasn't as warm as Roanoke, and I couldn't understand half my teammates, but I was enjoying the city and everything that came with it. I could definitely see myself living there. Steve told me that even though everything looked and sounded so rosy at Arsenal, it was incredibly difficult to make the first team, and the odds were heavily stacked against me. He wasn't trying to scare me, but he was being honest about the English footballing culture that is especially evident at larger clubs.

Once we were finished with dinner, Steve took us back to the hotel where I spent the night thinking about all the possibilities I'd been presented with in the past weeks. I'd hoped to come out of ESP camp with a nice scholarship that would have eased the burden of college costs for my parents. I'd done that. Schools from all over the country were contacting me with scholarship offers. Two weeks earlier, I'd never thought that the college of my choice might be competing with a top English club for my signature.

9. The trial part 2

The rest of the week of training was similar to the first two days. I started to see a pattern as the week progressed and enjoyed the warm up jog and tight one touch 4 v 2 or 5 v 2 possession games we played. Though all the work was serious and the players were in full concentration, a bit of fun could be had when defenders were nutmegged or caught running in circles as the outside players achieved up to ten and fifteen passes in a row. I also felt that, although it was so basic, these tight possession games always prepared my feet and mind for the session ahead.

The quick nature of the game as well as the extremely tight area we played in forced us to get physically as well as mentally up to speed. If a player was struggling to wake up for the session ahead, he'd find himself in the middle chasing the ball the whole time. No one wanted to be that guy. On top of constantly having to defend, the coach would walk around highlighting that you'd been in the middle for too long. Those little possession games never lied. You were either tuned in and ready for the session ahead, or your mind was elsewhere, probably still in bed.

The first team was involved in the Community Shield against Liverpool that Saturday, and I was excited to see them play after being involved with the club for roughly a week. The Community Shield is basically a way to kick off the season by matching up the previous year's League winners against the previous year's FA Cup winners. The reserves trained that Saturday morning, and then my dad and I headed back to the hotel to catch the game on TV. We watched as Gilberto scored the game-winning goal for Arsenal and then hopped on a train back into London for more sightseeing and relaxation.

My dad packed his bags that night and left early the next morning, as the plan was that he would only stay for the first week of the trial. It was tough seeing him leave because he seemed to be the only bit of reality I was experiencing in this dream land I was in. I also checked out of the hotel on Sunday and made my way over to my new "digs" for the upcoming week. When teams in England sign young players to academy contracts, they are usually put up with families that take care of them and act as parent figures to them. These accommodations are generally called "digs" and the family I would be staying with was already housing Sebastian Larsson, a Swede whose blue eyes and blonde hair made him look the part, and Ingi Hojsted, a boy from the Faroe Islands, a small set of islands north of the United Kingdom.

The house was three storeys tall with two bedrooms on the third floor for the players they housed. Ingi and Seb shared a room and, from what I could tell, had become good friends in the time they had been in London together. I had a room opposite but spent the majority of the time in their room, watching movies or playing Xbox. The three of us, despite being from different nooks and crannies of the world, meshed quite well, and it was nice having two familiar faces at the training ground the following week.

I quickly forgot about the loneliness I had felt when my dad left and enjoyed spending time with kids who were my age and living the life I was ultimately aiming for. The family I stayed with lived in a part of London called Barnet, where a number of the other digs were located. Seb, Ingi, and I would spend the afternoons playing pool with Patrick Cregg and Stephen O'Donnell, two Irish boys whose accents and personalities in general amused me. They told me what life was like living in London and playing football for such a big club. I knew right away that this lifestyle would definitely suit me and was happy that I had the chance to speak with these foreign boys about their experiences in England.

In my second week of training, I was much more comfortable and actually felt like a part of the team rather than an outsider. It made such a difference knowing some of the players' names and my training reflected it. I scored several goals in training and was really pleased with the way everything was going. After our sessions ended, some of the reserves would walk over to the first team pitch to watch the superstars train. I couldn't even begin to imagine what it would be like running alongside Thierry Henry or Dennis Bergkamp, trying to get past Ashley Cole, or trying to score on David Seaman.

Once again my questions were answered the following day. As all the reserves jogged out of the building towards the pitch we would be training on that day, a steady rain fell and grey clouds blanketed the North London sky. When we reached Eddie, he quickly said, "Danny, you are training with the first team today. Go and join up with them now." I wish someone had taken a picture of my face when his words registered in my brain because it probably would have been priceless. Several of my new "teammates" wished me luck and I started the two-minute jog towards the first team pitches. Everything was happening so fast, and I couldn't believe what I would be doing for the next hour and a half.

Looking back, this was probably for the best. If I had been told the evening before and given an entire night to sleep on it, I think I would have been too jittery to actually get any sleep. Of course, I was nervous when I met up with the first team, but I don't think anything could have prevented me feeling that way. In any line of work, when someone is given the opportunity to work with the most successful people in the field, certain levels of anxiety are necessary and expected.

As I rounded the bend that opened up to the first team pitches, I noticed all sorts of photographers, video cameramen, and journalists lined up behind a thin rope next to one of the side-lines on my left. When I crept into their peripheral vision, it was like a command had been shouted and every camera turned quickly and had me as the target. Apparently it was media day at the club, which was a big deal because it was the first and only day the media was allowed into the complex for video, interviews, and pictures. They must have thought I was some sort of big time signing that the Boss had somehow managed to keep a secret up until now. They didn't realise it was just me, Danny Karbassiyoon, a boy from Roanoke, Virginia, who was trying to comprehend everything that was taking place while trying to look as confident as he possibly could.

I joined the team on their routine jog around the pitches and listened contently as Arsenal's superstars made casual conversation. All around me, world class players jogged as if nothing was out of the ordinary. Roughly five World Cup winners (Gilberto, Vieira, Henry, Pires, and Wiltord) trained that day, but the accolades and achievements of the other players, both for club and country, could have filled a large auditorium. The team stretched and warmed up in similar fashion to the way I was used to warming up with the reserves. We did some short passing and played the possession game I had become accustomed to. This time, however, the quality of possession was slightly different. Imagine being in the middle and trying to get the ball when Thierry Henry, Dennis Bergkamp, Kanu, Patrick Vieira, and Robert Pires are all passing around you. Needless to say, the standard of possession was unbelievable, and the group I was in was sharper and quicker than anything I'd ever experienced.

It really isn't 'just' football anymore once you get to the highest level. This dynamic actually played through my mind several times after I'd signed permanently for Arsenal. I remember growing up and always playing with such freedom in my game. As mentioned, football was always a release for me. At the pro level, when contracts are signed, money is paid, and results are expected, it is different. Not necessarily different in a bad way, but different in that there is a lot more pressure to perform. At a club like Arsenal trialists would be brought in every so often, sometimes in your position. This would do all sorts to a player mentally. Am I not playing well enough right now? Are they really looking to replace me? I'd never experienced that sort of situation growing up in the States. It was certainly different, but it made me realise just how cut-throat the industry was. It made for more of a challenge, and I loved challenges.

After we finished our warm-up, the team and I made our way over to a circuit that Tony Colbert, the team's fitness coach, had set out. Miniature hurdles, speed ladders, mannequins, and elastic bands were purposefully placed in a grid, and we were told to partner up. I was standing next to Sol Campbell, one of the biggest and strongest *people,* never mind football players, that I had ever seen. His nod confirmed that we'd be partners, and we started the circuit soon after. A lot of emphasis was put on being as explosive as you could while being agile enough to maintain control of your body and the ball if there was one. The circuit was composed of a lot of quick, short exercises that were demanding physically, but not overly difficult; however, I began to worry when Sol and I moved on to the elastic band exercise.

Basically a player puts a belt around his waist with an elastic band attached to the back. The other player holds onto the band and provides some resistance as the player wearing the belt tries to sprint about twenty yards. It's a pretty simple exercise and when done the right way can build a lot of power and acceleration. I started to wonder about the physics of everything when Sol put the belt on. If someone is 6'4" and weighs 200 pounds, is it possible for a person who is 5'8" and weighs a measly 160 pounds to even be a factor when dealing with elastic bands and resistance? The answer, to be honest, is no. Sol took off down the field when Tony gave him the signal and I simply went along for the ride, trying everything I could to provide some sort of resistance to slow him down.

Nothing. Absolutely nothing. A couple of players had noticed and were amused at the sight of me flying down the pitch behind the powerhouse that was Sol Campbell.

I thought that was embarrassing. But I hadn't really thought about what happens when someone who is 6'4" and weighs 200 pounds tries to resist someone who is 5'8" and weighs 160 pounds as they run down the pitch. I soon found out. Strapped up and ready to go, I was determined to barrel down the pitch and impress the fitness coaches. Sol had other plans. When Tony gave us the signal, I exploded off the end line, only to find myself engaged in a stationary sprint. To my dismay, Sol was smirking behind me as I used every ounce of energy I had to go nowhere. Several of the players found it entertaining and were laughing before Sol eased up a little and let me complete the drill. I couldn't really be that upset. Sol Campbell was just joking around with me and had broken the metaphorical ice I had been standing on for the whole of the session. I was a bit more relaxed as we broke up into two teams and headed to the four goal pitch that was set up adjacent to the pitch we had just trained on.

The size of the pitch that had been set out for the following session was shockingly narrow. There were four goals (two on each end line) with goalkeepers occupying each of them. Once again, the game would emphasise tight control, quick thinking, and changing the point of attack. I picked up the bib my team was assigned and was delighted to see Thierry Henry pick one up as well. So I was joking with Sol in warm-ups and joining Thierry up front during the game? There were definitely no complaints coming from my end. I naturally drifted to the left when the game started, and Lauren, a fantastic right back from Cameroon, picked me up. To his left, Sol completed the two man wall that stood between me and David Seaman, who was keeper for Arsenal and the English National Team keeper at the time.

The game was very quick, and the two-touch limitation forced everyone to play much faster than I was accustomed to. The reserves had been a big step up from what I had become comfortable with in the States. The jump from the reserves to the first team was exponentially higher than the jump from the States to the reserves. The intensity of the session was unbelievably high, and it was a pleasure to see everyone working so hard but making it look so easy. One of the most alarming things was how much everyone spoke on the pitch. From the moment the ball kicked off, it sounded as if chaos had broken loose. *Controlled* chaos. "Force him outside!" "Bring him inside!" "Watch the runner!" "Tuck in!" "Left shoulder!" Defenders guided midfielders who guided the strikers who returned the favour. Everyone worked as a unit, and I learned quickly that Arsenal's defence was incredibly difficult to break down.

After maintaining possession several times for my team, I began to feel comfortable and started to express myself a bit more. I managed to score and even drew an apology from Thierry after he misplayed a ball during an attack on goal. Two goals were eventually removed and the game turned into a regular game on a shortened pitch. Thierry was remarkable in these games. His unlimited confidence fuelled him to take players on, make outrageous passes, and score breath-taking goals. Several times I had to snap out of it and realise these outrageous passes had me as the intended target. Soon after, the game and the training session came to an end. Several of the players headed back to the dressing rooms, but most stayed out to work on long balls or just shoot on the keepers. I made my way over to the Boss and thanked him for the opportunity and then headed back to the dressing room with a massive smile on my face.

I actually still laugh at what I did. At the time, I had no idea who recommended me to train with the first team that day – whether it was Steve Rowley, Eddie N., or the Boss himself. I grew up in a strict household and was raised to thank people when they did things for me. Regardless of who had asked me to train with the first team that day, the Boss had opened his team and session up to me and I was grateful for it. I knew it was a two-hour segment of my life that I'd never forget, no matter what happened in my career. All the cameras once again went straight to me when I did it, and I could hear the shutters clicking in the distance.

Steve met me in the cafeteria after I had showered and changed and asked me what I thought about the day. I was obviously ecstatic to have had the chance to play with the first team, and Steve told me that Lauren had told him that I was very good with both feet and, therefore, difficult to read when I got the ball. He also told me I wouldn't be training with the reserves the next day, and to rest up because I would be completing a series of fitness tests on my final day.

The final day of my trial was upon me and I was both happy and somewhat sad to see it come so quickly. I met up with Tony Colbert around 10 am and he told me to have a good breakfast and to meet him at the first team pitches in about an hour.

I completed several speed tests that involved me running through sensors spaced at different intervals and then had my jumping ability measured. After we finished up outside we headed to the gym and specifically one of the treadmills. Tony asked me to take my shirt off and strapped a heart rate monitor around my chest. The instructions for the next test were easy. Run until exhaustion. "Uh-oh," I thought as I stepped onto the treadmill. Tony informed me that I would warm up at a set pace for three minutes and then bump up to a fast jog and continue to increase the speed by half a mile per hour every three minutes. After roughly twenty minutes of running and finishing out at a straight sprint, my legs, heart, and lungs couldn't take it anymore. I jumped to the sides of the treadmill, gasping for air and wondering if my time was respectable. After one week at ESP camp, two weeks at Arsenal, and the infamous treadmill test, my body was basically screaming at me. I was definitely happy with my trial and knew that even if I wasn't offered a contract, I had done my best and given everything I could possibly have given.

I met with Steve later in his office. It was a comfortable space; his furniture, a desk, two couches, and an entertainment centre with a television used for watching DVDs of players, took up most of the room. Random knick-knacks from some of the trips he'd been on were scattered around. Ironically, a California license plate with the word "Arsenal" on it hung from the wall that faced his desk.

My birthday was the following day and Steve told me he had a gift for me; the club had had a brand new number nine "Karbassiyoon" shirt made with game shorts and socks to go with it. Every time I thought the surprises were over, another one would make its way to the surface. I think a lot of clubs that want to sign a certain player will do what it takes to make the player feel special. At 18, something as simple as my name on the back of one of the most famous shirts in the world was worth more than any amount of money.

Still excited to be holding Arsenal's latest kit with my name across the back, I was asked to sit down on the couch adjacent to Steve's desk. We briefly went over the week again, and he asked me how I felt about everything. What he said next was what I'd been hoping I'd eventually hear after I hung up the phone with him several weeks back when he initially invited me on trial. Steve told me that the club had decided to offer me a two year contract with an option of two more years. They would allow me to finish my senior year in high school, but I was to report back to London in December for a week's worth of training.

I couldn't believe it. I know I had told myself the entire time that I was going to get a contract and that I wouldn't leave without one, but actually hearing the words and seeing it on paper made it real. He also told me that I had a big decision to make, knowing very well that my education was a very big priority for me. A day later, I was sitting on a British Airways flight en route from Heathrow to Washington Dulles International Airport. With more on my plate than I had ever thought possible, I was heading home with a contract offer from one of the world's football powerhouses and a decision to make that could completely change the course of my life.

10. Decisions, decisions

The summer of 2002 was incredibly eventful and definitely one to remember. So much had changed for me, and I had a tough time comprehending how that one phone call that took me off the waiting list at ESP had literally transformed my future prospects. Not only had ESP brought the entire Arsenal experience with it, but I had been given the chance to play in front of hundreds of college coaches at the camp. Scholarship offers in the form of letters, emails, and phone calls started pouring in, and it was such a great feeling knowing I had so many options thanks to a simple game with two goals and a ball.

Even though I look back now and think what an easy decision it should have been to make regarding either going to Arsenal or going to college, it really wasn't that clear cut at the time. All my life I had wanted to go to college when I graduated from high school. I also dreamed of being a professional football player but didn't really worry about how that would happen. I always just assumed something would come up after college and I'd end up being a famous player with all sorts of endorsements and World Cup medals. Every boy's dream, right?

I didn't rush into any decisions and listened to a lot of college coaches on the phone. Almost every ACC school and Ivy League school showed a great amount of interest, and Virginia Tech's coach, Oliver Weiss, even drove up to Roanoke for a home visit to meet up with my dad and me. Oliver handed me a letter that night giving me the chance to be the first soccer player at Virginia Tech ever to be offered a full ride. I visited Duke and the University of Virginia on official visits and fell in love with both schools immediately. Not only was the soccer good at the institutions where I was being offered scholarships, but the educational opportunities I could potentially have received were unbelievable.

Once again, there were all sorts of factors being put into both options, and a lot of the coaches wanted to know my decision before December so they could focus their energy on recruiting other players if they had to.

On top of the major decision I was facing with football, the weight of my senior year of high school pressing down on my shoulders, and everything else a typical seventeen-year-old faces every day, my mother and I were working very hard to secure my Italian passport. Steve had asked me whether or not I was able to qualify for an Italian passport when I was in London during my first trial, and, because my mother was born in Naples and was as Italian as a hot dish of lasagne, my answer had been yes. Getting a work permit to live and play professionally in England is incredibly difficult, and with an Italian passport I would be classified as European and would have no problems. Unfortunately, skill alone doesn't enable players to sign for English clubs and the immigration offices in England have a set of tight rules they adhere to which prevent many players from signing. These rules include but aren't limited to:

- Players who are in possession of a European Union passport can be granted a work permit.
- Players who have featured in 75% of their full national team's games in the past two years (as long as that national team is ranked in FIFA's top 70) can be granted a work permit.
- Players who are deemed 'exceptional' and will make a huge impact in the League can be granted a work permit.

Although there are other ways to get access to a work permit, these are the main ways and the most frequently used.

The process that ensued once my mother and I were told we should start applying for my dual citizenship was more than painful. The nearest Italian Consulate to Roanoke was in Philadelphia, Pennsylvania, and we had to complete the eight-hour drive several times to fill out and sign papers. By no means did the Italians expedite the process, but after waiting almost eight months I was granted my Italian citizenship and thus given my work permit in the form of an Italian passport. Regardless of all the hassle, I was more than happy to have the document that would make playing in England a possibility for me.

As fall came and passed and my second one week trial with Arsenal in December approached, I started feeling a bit of pressure from the college coaches and realised I needed to make a decision. Obviously I didn't want to rule out anything until I had returned from England in December, so I did just that.

I was much more comfortable during my second trial at the club and used the trip to try to absorb as much about what my lifestyle would be like in roughly half a year. The first thing that I noticed on arrival in London was how wet, cold, and dark it seemed to be in the winter. The whole week I was there, a steady rain fell on London and darkness took over the sky as early as 3.30 pm on some days.

I was happy to see the staff again, and the friends I had made during the summer were receptive to me when they saw me in the dressing room on the first day.

This time I went straight into digs as opposed to the hotel. I was put into the care of Noreen Davies, one of the friendliest and most hospitable people I have ever met to this day. Patrick Cregg and Stephen O'Donnell, the two Irish kids I had met during my previous trial, were also staying with her, and we picked up right where we left off.

Noreen was and still is wonderful. I still keep in touch with her, her two sons and their wives and kids to this day. She's an older woman whose short stature and wonderfully warm smile can make anyone feel immediately at ease. A lifelong supporter of the Gunners, she has an incredible collection of matchday programmes from way back, and her house is decorated with memorable pictures of teams past. I honestly think she loves the club very much and enjoys being a part of it in a unique way. Some very special players like Philippe Senderos, Cesc Fabregas, Moritz Volz, and Sebastian Svard have spent time at her house, and I think she takes huge pride in that. To the boys that stay with her, she's a mother first and a fan second.

On the football side of the trial, training was just as I remembered. Each work-out was physically demanding and seemed even harder because of the weather conditions. The pitches were all still in pristine condition, but the wet conditions seemed to speed up the pace of the games and also made slide tackles much more appealing. The reserves were full swing into their season and actually had an away game against Coventry City scheduled while I was in town. I was allowed to travel with the team and enjoyed the experience. The game was at Highfield Road, Coventry's former stadium, and players like Kolo Toure, Sebastian Svard, and Sebastian Larsson all enjoyed a run out. Kolo was still trying to break into the first team as a regular at that point, but anyone could tell that his ability and commitment to the game were exceptional.

Even though the training and reserve team games were both enjoyable and very educational for me, the highlight of the trip came in the middle of the week. In fact, I had been looking forward to the middle of that week since Steve had booked my flight roughly a month earlier. On December 11th, 2002 Sebastian Svard and I picked up Kolo Toure before heading to Highbury for Arsenal's Champions League match against Valencia of Spain. As we took our seats in the paddock, the section of seats right behind the players' bench, I stared in amazement all around me. I thought seeing the stadium was a spectacular sight in the summer when it was just my dad, Steve, and me there. I had no idea that it could be made into an even more spectacular sight by adding 38,500 screaming, singing fans with twenty two players on the pitch.

I felt like a tourist with my camera, snapping pictures and taping short video clips, but I definitely wanted to take the night home with me in some form. The Champions League theme song played as the teams filed out of the tunnel and lined up. The crowd roared as Arsenal's team was announced one by one: Seaman, Lauren, Cygan, Campbell, Cole, Ljungberg, Vieira, Gilberto, Pires, Bergkamp, and Henry. Names like Aimar, Angulo, Baraja, and Carew made up Valencia's team, and their travelling supporters made themselves heard in the Clock End.

The game ended in a 0-0 draw, but the result wasn't the biggest thing occupying my mind. The final whistle marked the end of the game, but the beginning of a new chapter for me. After watching the game, hearing the crowd, and soaking in the electric atmosphere, I knew I belonged in England. I called my dad after the game and stumbled over my words trying to describe the ninety minutes I had just seen. Hearing about the game he was almost as excited as I was and was also pleased and supportive when I told him I was going to take Arsenal up on the offer and move to England after I graduated from high school. When I was done rambling on about everything that had happened that night, my dad somehow managed to make my night even better. He told me the US Soccer Federation had called inviting me to the U18 National Team's next camp in Chula Vista, California at the beginning of January.

I was so relieved to have made it through my second trip to Arsenal. The weight of the biggest decision of my life had been eased off my shoulders, and I would be representing my country at a national team camp for the first time in a couple of weeks. Everything was perfect. My knee felt great, my confidence was at an all-time high, and I was excited about every aspect of my life.

The day before I returned home from England, I told Steve and the club that I would be taking them up on their offer and would not be going down the college route. They were very excited to hear about my decision, and I was equally excited to tell them. I returned home and started making phone calls to the many college coaches who had been trying hard to recruit me.

My junior and senior years of high school were incredibly unique in that I'd never been courted so heavily by multiple institutions/teams. Some of the schools sent me letters every single week of my junior year and then called me every week of my senior year (the NCAA rules only allowed written correspondence as a junior and then allowed phone calls once a week as a senior). I'd established relationships with several college coaches who had shown faith in me and offered me those wonderful scholarships before Arsenal had even come into the picture. Duke's assistant coach, for example, had sent me multiple handwritten letters throughout my junior year, arranged a preliminary "unofficial visit" for my father and me, and then called nearly every week of my senior year. Out of courtesy I felt the need to express my thanks to these coaches and schools for having so much belief in me. I also wanted to make sure they could adjust their recruiting plans to not include me.

A lot of the coaches were disappointed, but most were happy that I had made the decision to take Arsenal up on a once-in-a-lifetime opportunity. In fact, a lot of the coaches jokingly made me promise that if they ever came to England I would have to provide them with tickets to an Arsenal game!

Another great perk that came along with agreeing to go professional was Adidas' offer to sign me to a sponsorship contract. They contacted me immediately after they caught wind of my trial with Arsenal and consistently sent me various pieces of kit throughout the months leading to my final decision. As soon as I decided to no longer pursue the college option, I was able to forego my amateur status and signed my first endorsement deal. When a player with amateur status, for example, a high school or college athlete, signs any sort of contract with an agent, team, or company that represents them, the athlete immediately loses his amateur status and eligibility and is unable to play in college due to the rules set forth by the National Collegiate Athletic Association, or NCAA.

When I finally did sign with them, I was sent more football boots than I had ever seen at one time, along with running shoes, shorts, socks, shirts, and a bunch of other things for my family. I was given a certain amount of money that I was able to spend on casual wear for myself and my family. At the time, Adidas provided an online catalogue where I could sign on and pick out whatever I wanted, compile a list, and send it to my rep. I didn't even have to go the store!

Along with the Adidas and Arsenal contracts came phone calls from various agencies looking to secure my signature as well. Will Sherling, an agent from the IMG group, flew to Roanoke to meet with my family and me. Although he was English, he was living in the United States at the time, but I was hesitant to sign with an agent who would be so far away from me once I signed my contract in England. I spoke to several other agencies on the phone and was also told by Steve Rowley that I could use an agent used by a lot of the players at Arsenal to simply negotiate my contract. Steve explained that if I liked the work the agent did for me, then I could sign with him once it was all said and done. I decided to follow Steve's advice and didn't sign with anyone until nearly a half a year into my contract, when Will Sherling was transferred to London and captured my signature.

There were certainly agents whom I both liked and disliked. I met with several of them before deciding that Will was the right guy. Will made my dad and me feel as if we actually mattered, whereas some agents were more preoccupied with telling us that they represented massive players and were indeed big-time themselves. All that did to my dad and me was let us know that those particular agents wouldn't have time for me. The agent world is definitely murky but they are completely necessary. Many are lawyers or have lawyers in their agencies who specialise in looking over contracts and making sure everything is above board. Without them, players would struggle to navigate through all the legal documents highlighting clauses, triggers, bonuses, and all the good stuff that makes up professional sports contracts. Good agents are well connected and can promote their clients in positive ways. They obviously make more money when their player makes more money, so their judgement can sometimes be questioned when a player's future is at stake. What brings the agent more money may not necessarily be the right move for the player.

My senior year of high school continued, and I was called into several more domestic national team camps before taking part in my first international event at a tournament in France with the U18s in May of 2003. I really enjoyed my time with the national team and made a lot of good friends like Brad Guzan, Greg Dalby, Adam Cristman, Hunter Freeman - all players who went on to become professionals themselves: Guzan (Aston Villa), Greg Dalby (Colorado Rapids), Adam Cristman (LA Galaxy), Hunter Freeman (Colorado Rapids).

Knowing that I was playing with the top players in the country in my age group and representing the entire United States in a foreign country filled me with pride and satisfaction. I loved playing for my country, and every time I put the red, white, and blue shirt on and saw the US badge sitting over my heart, I knew it was special. Before games I'd always look at the badge and think, "out of all the kids playing soccer in our country, I've been selected to be in the top eleven." It was empowering and humbling all at once.

Because school was so important to me, I had to leave France a day early in order to be back in Roanoke for my high school graduation. I was always so competitive in school with everything I did and ended up being one of the valedictorians of my graduating class with a 4.2 out of 4.0 GPA. I had heard of so many athletes finishing their careers early because of injury or other reasons and not having anything to fall back on and definitely did not want to fall into that boat. A lot of my teachers couldn't comprehend how I could possibly pass on college to pursue some "soccer thing" in England, but they obviously didn't understand that the "thing" I was going to be chasing was the thing I had been dreaming of my whole life.

Just like that, my senior year of high school had come to an end and with it came the end of a massive chapter of my life. My final game in the United States was both a humbling and proud experience, to say the least. After being selected to the McDonald's All American game several weeks earlier, I made my way to Charleston, South Carolina, to participate in the three day event that culminated in the big game on the final day. All the best high school seniors in the country were present at the game, including my friend and fellow Roanoker, Drew Harrison.

The timing of the game couldn't have been better. All the seniors whom I had graduated with earlier in the month were celebrating in Myrtle Beach, South Carolina, and a big group of my friends made the short trip to see the game and cheer me on. Unfortunately for the Eastern team, Kenny Cooper and Vedad Ibišević, two players who went on to have excellent careers themselves, led the West to a 6-1 drubbing. Regardless of the result, I was happy to have made the game and very pleased to take part in all the community activities that surrounded the three day weekend.

I enjoyed the final month and a half I had at home with my friends and family, but made sure to get as fit as I possibly could for the start of pre-season. While all my friends were preparing for their college careers, I was packing my bags for my five-and-half-thousand-mile journey across the world and couldn't wait finally to be starting the life I had been anticipating for so long.

11. What it means to be a Gunner

Two days after celebrating America's independence in Roanoke, I was back in London and ready to start pre-season for the first time as a professional. The club had found a nice two bedroom apartment for me in Enfield, but it wasn't completely furnished yet, and Mortiz Volz, my good German friend and one of Arsenal's right backs, and his girlfriend Anneke were kind enough to put me up while I waited for everything to be put in order. I was happy to see familiar faces again, and it helped keep my mind off everyone I had left back home. Both Sebastians, Moritz, Ingi, and the Irish boys all had several years left on their contracts, so a majority of the friends I had made on my two previous trips were still associated with the club. When I arrived at the training ground for the first day of training, though, I was surprised to see that not everyone I had trained with the year before was still there.

The process of making it to Arsenal's first team from the youth and reserve set up is incredibly difficult. Although most of the clubs in England have age groups starting from as young as nine, it's not until players turn sixteen that they officially join the club's Academy books. Obviously, if a player has excelled in his age group and is good enough to play with the older boys, then he can be bumped up until the coaches and staff feel the player is getting the most benefit from his peers.

The U18 team is the official Academy Team, and players on the team are considered a part of the Youth Training Scheme, or YTS. YTS players earn a very small weekly wage and continue their schooling through the club. If players are good enough to earn their first contract, they will be considered a reserve team player and earn a considerable increase in pay. Some players, like Theo Walcott for example, sign professional forms and head directly to the first team dressing room. Schooling then becomes optional with football being the main priority. From there, players compete for spots in the reserve team with the ultimate goal of training with and making the first team. From roughly the thirty players that made up the reserves while I was at Arsenal, four players were offered second contracts and the rest were released. One of those players, Cesc Fabregas, went on to become Arsenal's captain before Barcelona came calling several years later.

With that said, a number of the boys I had seen on my previous trips were no longer at the training ground. Some had been released, some had been sent out on loan, while some had been transferred to other teams during the transfer window. Just like everything else, though, new faces replaced the old ones, and pre-season was underway.

I wasn't too surprised by all the endurance, speed, agility, and stamina work the fitness coaches had set up for us. I had dealt with quite a bit during my trial and I had spent the majority of my time building up my fitness levels in the months leading to

61

pre-season. We engaged in a lot of interval and station training where we would work hard for a set amount of time on one exercise, rest, and then change exercises. Both reserve and first team players were mixed together during pre-season, so it was always a great opportunity to impress the Boss and the rest of the first team staff. We'd usually go through the entire circuit once or twice and then move on to more fitness. All the players were determined to impress, and the goal of all the fringe players was to get invited on to the pre-season tour to Austria.

In terms of rest – a key part of the player experience - I slept well also! I'd usually come home from training around two o'clock or so and take a nap in the afternoon for an hour or so. Nearly all of us did that. I'd go up to Sebastian Larsson's flat to play PlayStation or watch television and wake up on his couch a couple of hours later. Seb would be fast asleep on the other couch. The weather in London made sleeping exceptionally pleasant for me. I'd crack a window open, let the cool air in, and fall asleep to the rain falling outside. It wasn't hard at all!

The first two weeks of pre-season were hell. Double sessions were the norm and I quickly learned that recovering was just as important as working hard. Every day we'd start training around 10.30 am and work solely on fitness until roughly 12.30 pm. Mini trampolines, medicine balls, and cones flooded the pitches. We worked on our jumping ability, acceleration, balance, core strength, endurance, and power throughout the morning session and then did a warm-down, stretch and headed inside to take showers, get massages, and get treatment if we needed it. A new training kit would be ready for us, and after showering and changing we'd get lunch upstairs and then rest for an hour or so before heading back out to the fields. The food that "Chef" prepared was top class and varied daily. An entire buffet of meats, fish, steamed vegetables, greens, and fruit welcomed us every day, with soups as appetizers, and yogurt and pies for desserts. Everything was made with nutrition and performance in mind, but was also totally delicious. Afternoon sessions were like a breath of fresh air because we actually got to use balls. A lot of the teams in England don't even get to use balls for the first two weeks because the coaches think fitness is all that pre-season is about. I think that getting the chance to use them in the afternoon, when the players are feeling their muscles and joints ache and are ready to just lie down and call it a day, is crucial. It helps train players to be able to play in the final third of games, when both muscles and minds start slowing due to exhaustion.

After another hour or hour and a half of football in the afternoon the day would come to an end, and the players would head home to rest in preparation for a repeat the following day. The same schedule stuck from Monday through Saturday, and the occasional day would be thrown in where we would only have one session. I didn't realise just how sore I was until after the first week of work. I was walking down the street with Brett Lemon, one of my best friends who had moved over to London with me for the first six months to pretty much work and have fun, and we were talking about how everything was going so far. He laughed at me as I explained to him how I'd never been so sore in all my life. With every step I took, all of my leg, arm, and core muscles screamed at me. No matter how much work I had done by myself, nothing prepared me for the sheer volume and intensity of the work I had completed that week.

Several weeks into pre-season, I was delighted to be informed by the club that I had been called into the U18 US National Team that would be travelling to Northern Ireland to compete in the Milk Cup. Because players are employed by their club teams and not national teams, the clubs are given the right to release or retain players for national team duty. Although I had only been in London for roughly a month, I was thrilled to get the call up and couldn't wait to meet up with my American teammates in Northern Ireland. Our first group game of the tournament had us matched up against Poland, and my late header levelled the score line and earned us a well-deserved point.

Our next opponent, Paraguay, ended up actually beating Brazil in the final and proved to us why they were the best team in the tournament. It only took about three minutes for them to score, and never had I been on a team that was played off the park so badly. This particular Paraguayan team was on a different level from our US team. It was obviously an upsetting experience to lose in an international tournament, but it was also extremely educational. Right from the get go I could tell we were in for a tough match. The Paraguayan captain was screaming at his teammates in the tunnel, getting them completely psyched up for the match, while we kind of just stood next to them in the tunnel with blank looks on our faces. We looked to our captain for some sort of war-cry but I think he was as intimidated as the rest of us. When we lost, we were upset but we knew we'd been beaten by a team that was not only better than us, but also wanted it more than us. Needless to say, our national team coach made that very clear to us.

We regrouped in the final group game, beating Scotland 2-0 while securing a spot in the third and fourth place game in the process. My second goal of the tournament, a right-footed volley from Arturo Alvarez's corner, came in the final minutes against Scotland and was enough to secure the Golden Boot for the competition. After playing in an uneventful draw against Denmark that left us as winners after a penalty shootout, the trip came to an end, and it was time for me to make my way back to London. I was pleased with my performance at the tournament and was thrilled to have won the top goal scorer award in the process. Most of all, however, the week away from London helped break up the monotony of pre-season and left me ready for the season ahead.

As pre-season came to a close, the Boss narrowed down his list of first teamers who would be involved in the tour to Austria. Track suits, travel polos, running shoes, sandals, and massive winter bench jackets were distributed to everyone, and training continued. I wasn't chosen to travel with the first team, and those reserves who also weren't chosen stayed in London, played several pre-season friendlies at the training ground, and then flew to Belgium to compete against Beveren, a team in the Belgian League. When the first team returned from Austria, they would generally play in one or two pre-season tournaments for the final preparation for the beginning of the Premiership.

Although I knew pre-season was taking a toll on my body physically, I was still not really aware of just how much work I had put myself through in my first month in England. With roughly two-thirds of pre-season gone, I was called into camp with the U20 US National Team. Thomas Rongen had named an 18 man roster that would be taking part in a tournament just outside Valencia in Spain, and Frankie Simek and I both made the short journey down to the Iberian Peninsula to meet up with the team. My groin was slightly sorer than the rest of my battered body, but I didn't think anything of it and played in all five games of the tournament. Guys like Clint Dempsey, Chad Marshall, and Drew Moor all featured in the team, and we ended up finishing third in the tournament. As the tournament progressed, however, my groin became more and more painful to the point that it was almost unbearable for me to play.

Once the tournament had ended Frank and I returned to London, and I started to get treatment on my groin. After a week or so of both treatment and stretching, I saw little improvement and was sent to see a specialist. Although the medical staff at Arsenal is extremely knowledgeable, players are outsourced to see specialists and get scans when pain persists or if injuries are unclear or very bad. I was diagnosed with a sport's hernia, specifically a Gilmore's groin (named after the doctor in London who performs the procedure to fix it), and was scheduled for surgery in a week. Basically, I had a slight tear in my groin and the operation would make my groin much stronger than it had been before. I informed my parents, and they scheduled their flight to come and help me around my flat while I was temporarily immobile.

I had surgery on September 11th, 2003 and spent the night in the hospital contemplating my luck with injuries. I was told that my recovery time would be roughly six weeks, but I wanted to be out with the team, training and preparing for the season ahead. The start of both the reserve season as well as the Premiership fell within the six week lay-off I was dealing with, and I was very frustrated.

When one is trying to make a career as a professional athlete, the two biggest setbacks are injuries and slumps in form. So far, during my two month tenure in London, I had not been playing the way I knew I could, and I was now facing an extended amount of time on the side-lines due to injury.

I followed the physio's protocol for rehab and was back with the reserves at the six week mark. The six weeks of rehab were full of core-strengthening exercises as well as cardiovascular work to keep my fitness levels high. I faced double sessions every day and couldn't wait for my body to heal so I could get back to training.

The season was in full swing at that point, which meant we had reserve games every Monday night. I soon became accustomed to the schedule of a typical week in the reserves:

- **Monday:** Depending on whether the game was home or away, we would meet at the training ground between 12.30 and 2 for a light training session and meal. Whether or not you were involved in that night's match depended on your name being on the sixteen-man list that was posted in the dressing room. The reserve team manager would name the starting eleven during the short session, and after a light jog we would go through set pieces and then head back in to shower and get ready for the game. Pre-match meals consisted of high protein and carbohydrate foods like eggs, beans, toast, spaghetti, and boiled or grilled chicken. From the training ground we would take the coach to the stadium, play the game, and then return to the training ground, grab our cars and head home.

- **Tuesday**: If a player had played over 45 or 60 minutes in a game, they would be excused from training and just take part in the warm-down. Those players warming down would ride a stationary bike for twenty minutes and then go through a series of stretches before calling it a day. The rest of the players who were on the bench, played too few minutes to qualify for the warm-down, or were left out of the squad completely, would train as usual with the reserve team manager.

- **Wednesday**: Usually a day off. If you were injured, your only day off would most likely be Sunday. Injured players nearly always had double sessions, with treatment being administered in the morning and light gym or pool work in the afternoon. As players began to feel better, they would start training outside with Tony Colbert and the rest of the fitness coaches before finally being approved to join back in regular training.

- **Thursday**: Training was usually the most demanding on Thursdays and Fridays. The session would usually last an hour and a half or two hours. The theme of the session (i.e. defending as a team, defending as a back four, attacking, finishing) determined what we would do in training. We'd usually finish the session with a small-sided game to goal and a series of fitness exercises to maintain our endurance and stamina.

- **Friday**: The phrase "Thank God it's Friday" never really came to mind on Fridays because we'd spend the first portion of our day in the gym and then head outside to do more agility and fitness work with the fitness coaches. Sessions would last up to two hours and leave everyone exhausted from the week's work.

- **Saturday**: The beginning of the weekend was just like any other day of training and the actual day usually lasted much longer if the first team had a home game. Training was relatively fun on Saturdays, because those first team players that were left out of the squad for that day's game would train with the reserves. Depending on injuries and players being left out, every week provided players like Edu, Vieira, Aliadière, Ljungberg, and many others. We'd usually play a small-sided game as the main portion of the session and then finish up with a crossing and finishing exercise. If the first team had a home game, Seb Larsson, Ingi Hojsted and I would head back to our flats, change into a suit and tie, and take the Piccadilly Line from Oakwood station to the Arsenal station. Attending home games was and still is mandatory for reserve and youth team players. After getting our tickets in the Marble Halls we'd make our way to our assigned seats which were located in the paddock, the small group of seats located behind the home bench and to the right of the players' tunnel. Kick-off was usually at 3pm, and the game would end by five, getting us back to our apartments by 6 o'clock.

• **Sunday**: There was usually a 95% chance that we would have Sunday off unless the first team had a Champions League game the following week and needed players to train with before they travelled. If the first team had a home game on a Sunday we would make our way to Highbury just as if it were a Saturday.

Despite being in England since the beginning of July it wouldn't be until mid-November that I would finally represent Arsenal officially in a reserve team game. I had been an unused substitute against Watford FC and Wimbledon FC after returning from my groin injury and on November 24th, 2003 was named as one of the starting strikers against Southampton FC. It wasn't a very eventful game by any means, and Southampton actually ended up winning 1-0 in the end, but the fact that I started, played 73 minutes, and had made my reserve team debut was a huge step for me.

It was a great experience being a part of the starting eleven, as my whole preparation for the game was dramatically different from when I was on the bench. Before walking out of the tunnel to start the game, the starters would go over their jobs on set pieces for and against. For example, when a ball went out and we were defending a corner, everyone already knew who would be on the near and far posts, who would be covering the hole, who would go out to the ball if they played a short corner, who was meant to cover the top of the box, and who was meant to be man marking. If one person failed to do their job correctly, the other team had a much higher chance of scoring on the set piece.

It didn't really matter whether it was a first team game or a reserve game, both physical and mental preparation was crucial. Obviously players would do everything they could physically to make sure they were well-rested and loose before games. Mentally it was important to get ready for the ninety minutes ahead by putting everything else in your mind aside and concentrating solely on what you had to do for the next hour and a half. At the highest levels of sport an opposing team usually has the ability to punish you if you slip up either mentally or physically for even a split second.

Training continued as normal, and I became accustomed to the training week and Monday night games. All our home games were played at Barnet FC's former stadium, the Underhill. As of 2015 Barnet competes in League 2, England's fourth division, and has since moved on from the Underhill Stadium. Arsenal used to have an agreement with Barnet which allowed the reserves to play all their home games at their ground. In return, Arsenal would also visit the Underhill in a pre-season friendly on a yearly basis. The game was always highly anticipated by both Arsenal and Barnet fans alike and drew large crowds excited to see both new signings and old stars ahead of the new season.

The stadium, which seats roughly 6,000 people, is located at the bottom of a slight hill, but the most interesting feature everyone notices when walking into the stadium is the slight slope that is visually obvious from the north to south end. Whoever was captaining the reserves on any given game night would be forced to decide whether to go uphill in the first half and have an easier second half or to try to use the hill as an advantage in the first half and just deal with the hill in the second half!

Every week was like a try-out. If I was training well and playing well in the games, then I'd have a great chance of being involved in the reserve team games on Monday. Out of a pool of roughly thirty players only sixteen could be chosen to dress for matches, meaning a good number of players were left out of the squad altogether. Although every player in the reserves and at the club always wanted to win, results weren't always the main priority in the reserves. If we had been working on something all week in training and demonstrated an understanding of that concept in the game on Monday but still lost, the staff and players would take the positives from the game and we'd put the loss behind us. The ultimate goal in the reserves is to develop players who can break into the prestigious first team, and both losses and wins in the reserve league are all part of the learning curve.

A specific game I remember where this was the case took place on a cold night in November of my second year at the club. I had been working on stopping crosses and preventing wide players from beating me in 1 v 1 situations all week prior to the game. Even though we lost to Norwich City at Carrow Road 2-1 that night, I didn't let any crosses in from my side and was impossible to get by in isolated situations. Neil Banfield, our reserve manager, was very upset with the way the whole team played and with the result, but took me aside after the game and commended me on both my defensive and attacking efforts.

After making my reserve team debut in November, I found myself in and out of the squad and ended up making eight starts and two substitute appearances throughout the season. It was especially frustrating getting to play one week and then completely being left out of the team the following week. I had always been one of the top players on my team growing up and finding myself on the bench or in the crowd troubled me mentally. I was over all my injuries and expected to be on the pitch every week and eventually started questioning my ability because I wasn't seeing results.

This feeling of 'failure' only motivated me more and more as the season continued. I usually stayed out after training had ended, working on longer driven balls, finishing, and other parts of my game that I wanted to improve. I would get into training earlier to use the gym for basic strengthening and short core work-outs. I knew I wasn't playing better than the current group of players who were getting to start week in and week out, and I wanted that to change. I wanted my daily soccer experience to go back to the way it was when I was at home, playing in my backyard and with my friends. I wanted to enjoy training and look forward to games, instead of worrying what my first touch would be like and whether or not I would pass it to the right team. My confidence was lower than it had ever been before, and being across the Atlantic Ocean and by myself didn't make matters easier. The most frustrating part was that I KNEW I wasn't playing anywhere near the level I was accustomed to and just couldn't figure out why. I soon realised that when you're having trouble believing in yourself, having someone else believe in you and trust you may be the only way to gain your own self-belief back.

A week before our away fixture against Watford's reserves on April 7th, Nicky Nicolau, our starting left-back, went out on loan because his contract was up at the end of the season and he wanted to begin his search for a new club. Eddie pulled me aside before training and told me he'd be playing me as a left-back in training for the week. I found it strange at first, but began getting more and more comfortable as the week went on. When match time rolled around on Monday night at Vicarage Road, I was wearing the number three shirt. (In England the numbers 1-11 all have positional significance. The following is a list of numbers and their respective positions: 1 – Goalkeeper, 2 – Right-Back, 3 – Left-Back, 4 – Centre Midfield, 5 – Centre-Back, 6 – Centre-Back, 7 – Right Midfield, 8 – Centre Midfield, 9 – Striker, 10 – Striker, 11 – Left Midfield.) My parents had come over to visit and I was extremely excited about playing in front of them. Eddie told me to relax and enjoy myself before the game started and encouraged me to listen and talk to Ollie Skulason, an Icelandic centre-back who played alongside me, as much as possible. He also explained that my assignment for the first five minutes was to figure out which foot Watford's right midfielder favoured, what his strengths were, what his weaknesses were, and whether or not he could use his pace to get past me. All this information would make the remaining eighty-five minutes much easier for me if assessed correctly. I ended up playing the full ninety, and the game ended in a 0-0 draw, which I was very happy with from a defensive standpoint.

The away fixture at Watford marked an important change for me. Not only was the monotony of training broken by me constantly having to learn new aspects of my new position, but I started looking forward to training again and was determined to master my positioning, defending, and attacking at left-back. I started the final three games of the season, which saw us host both Portsmouth and West Ham United and have a trip to Wimbledon. Every game presented new situations to me in my new position, and every week in training these new situations would be addressed and explained by Eddie. I quickly started learning what I was good at and what needed improving on. Needless to say, after having scored goals as my job for roughly fifteen years, trying to stop them from being scored wasn't what I'd call a strength of mine.

Even though the reserve season wrapped up nearly a month prior to the end of the Premiership's actual close, all the players were required to stay until the final game of the first team's season. We continued training and at the end of the season completed several fitness tests which would be used as a basis for comparison on our return the following season. The final game of the Premiership was incredibly special for everyone associated with Arsenal, because the first team managed to go the entire season unbeaten. Out of 38 League games played the Gunners had managed to win 26, draw 12, and lose 0. Accomplishing this feet in any league is impressive, but having done it in the Premiership, against some of the toughest competition in the world, was unbelievable. Since then, no team in England's top flight has managed to do what Arsenal did in the 2003-2004 season. Despite the influx of cash into the modern game, Wenger's record that season remains intact and will likely remain so for quite some time.

A day or two after Arsenal beat Leicester 2-1 at Highbury on the last day of the season, winning yet another Premiership trophy, I was on a plane heading back across the Atlantic. I was ecstatic to be going home and really needed a break from my first season as a pro. I was both mentally and physically drained, having visited home for only seven days during the Christmas period since moving to England in July. A fitness programme had been given to us which allowed us to take two weeks off before starting what was basically a "pre" pre-season training regimen. I was given roughly a month and a half off, and it felt strange not to be working out and playing soccer for the first two weeks. After my two week lay-off, I began running again and working out at the gym per the programme Tony Colbert had given me.

12. Off the field

My first year at Arsenal had been a trying one, but I learned a great deal about football, life, and myself in a very short period of time. Adjusting to life in London was one of the hardest and strangest things I'd ever done. While in the States I was accustomed to getting home from school around three o'clock on a daily basis, practising by myself in my backyard, practising with my team at night, doing my homework and spending time with my family. In England I found it odd adjusting to the fact that by 2 o'clock every day any concrete commitments were essentially done, and I had the rest of the day to do whatever I wanted. Spending time with my family came in the form of a five to ten minute phone call every other day or so. Homework no longer consisted of history, literature, and maths books sprawled across a desk. Instead, my attention was directed towards watching Premier League, La Liga, and Champions League matches. Watch the best, learn from the best, become the best.

It didn't take long for Seb, Ingi, and I to become close. For seventeen- and eighteen-year-olds it seemed that all it took to bond was an Xbox, the latest edition of FIFA, and eight hours of downtime every day. We'd almost become a clique within the reserves – the Irish boys all gravitated towards one another, the English generally did their own thing, and the "others" made sure to stick together and watch each other's backs. We were more than just teammates, and for me the feeling of brotherhood was essential. We'd travel into London almost once a week to shop, eat, and just walk around, but the forty-five minute tube ride, the crowded streets, and the cold damp air didn't make leaving the comfort of our flats in Enfield always that appealing.

One of the big differences I had to deal with upon arriving in London was my lack of a car. I'd been driving for almost three years in the States, but the thought of getting behind the wheel of a car with the steering wheel on the right-hand side seemed very daunting to me. I was heavily dependent on rides everywhere from club officials and teammates, but didn't particularly like always having to rely on someone to get me around. On my trials I'd become good friends with both Moritz and Sebastian Svard, and they were kind enough to provide these services until both of them went out on loan at the end of pre-season. Kolo Toure then offered me rides, and I quite enjoyed zooming down the Ridgeway in Enfield in his silver Toyota Celica while he blasted African dance music.

Eventually the time came, though, and Paul Irwin, the club's Player Liaison, advised that it was about time I took the plunge and got a car. As an American coming from the land of excess, where everything is bigger, the roads are wider, and the answer is always more power, I was excited about going car shopping. To hear Paul recommend the Ford Fiesta Zetec, a 1.4 litre hatchback that in a nutshell just looked weird to me, was disheartening. I asked Paul if he wouldn't mind continuing the search. Paul's rebuttal was sobering.

"You're already going to have to pay just over $4,500 for your yearly insurance premium with the Fiesta. Anything more powerful or sportier is going to blow your insurance out of the water."

"But I'm a footballer now. One that plays for Arsenal – surely I can get a nicer car."

"The moment you put Arsenal down as your employer, the insurance company is going to take into account that you could be driving around with Thierry or Patrick at any given time."

"But I've been driving for three years and haven't been in an accident."

"That's great Danny – you still have to put Arsenal down as your employer, though."

"Okay. Fiesta it is."

I suppose it made sense. In my second year at the club, after making several first team appearances one of my teammates decided to upgrade his car and bought a new six series BMW convertible. He also had to part with nearly 10,000 pounds for the insurance to cover him.

I had to wait a couple of weeks for my car to be ready, but I was ecstatic and couldn't wait for the day it was going to be delivered to my flat or the training ground. After a midweek training session sometime in October of 2003, Paul rang and informed me that my car was ready and available for collection. I was a bit confused because I was under the impression that it was to be delivered, but I didn't think much about it. About an hour later, my friend Brett and I were in Paul's car driving into central London to the private dealer.

Due to the lack of space in London, car dealerships aren't generally found in massive Auto-Mall settings as they are in the States. In central London there are no huge parking lots with thousands of cars. Instead, the dealerships make do with the room they are blessed with, strategically parking cars in their showrooms while limiting the inventory.

It took nearly thirty minutes to get to the dealership – Paul had been a driver prior to his role as Player Liaison and effortlessly navigated his way through the traffic, the tight roads, and everything else that made London an intimidating place for me to drive. He pulled into a tight driveway off a small street that led to a garage. Sitting at the top of the driveway was my brand new, navy blue Fiesta. I didn't really care what type of car it was anymore. More than anything I was pretty proud of myself for having made my first big purchase with my own money.

I signed all the papers and was handed the keys to my car. Paul smiled and told me I could follow him back to Enfield. Hold on. What do you mean "follow you back? Who is doing the driving?"

"You are, Danny. I'll show you the way and get you guys home."

Brett looked at me – a look of terror and confusion combined into one. He didn't need to say anything because I knew what he was thinking. *No way I'm getting in that car if you are driving.*

I didn't need to say anything either. Brett was able to decipher my look as well. *I don't blame you. I wouldn't get in the car with me, either.*

I suppose he could have ridden back with Paul, but we knew our thirty-minute drive home was going to be worthy of a good story someday. He uneasily opened the passenger door, contemplated his last chance at safety, and plopped in next to me. We agreed to a no-music, complete-focus-on-the-road ride back to Enfield, and I told Brett he'd have to help me with my distances on the left side of the car as I focused on changing gears with my left hand and on the road ahead.

I only scraped the curb twice on the way home and couldn't believe that I had not only driven in England, but that I'd also managed to avoid killing any pedestrians en route. The car definitely gave me a sense of freedom that I didn't have before. Within a week, I was comfortable driving to training, the local cinema, the grocery store, and Enfield's town centre. I was also able to repay other players with rides home and began spending more time with Philippe Senderos and Cesc Fabregas as I was able to drive to their digs. All the foreigners were in a similar boat: away from home, away from friends and family, and away from everything we were so used to. Many of our discussions cantered around our hometowns, our friends, and our cultures. I remember one specific night when Philippe and I spent about two hours on Google Earth zooming in on different parts of Geneva and Roanoke describing and showing each other everything there was to know about each place. Talk about worlds apart!

Despite spending a good amount of time with my teammates, the majority of my time was spent in my flat by myself. I knew from the start of my time in the UK that treating my body well would be essential to a prolonged career, and I made sure I was doing everything I could to put in solid shifts at training every day. I soon learned that spending a majority of my time on the couch, in my bed, or by my computer was the best way for me to recover and prepare for whatever the next day had in store for me. It was certainly lonely at times, an odd concept considering I was in a city of eleven million, fulfilling my dream with the world's best young and senior players. I often wondered what my friends were doing at home, what my family had planned for the weekend, and even what my life might have been like had I opted to stay in the States and go to college instead. At times I envied my teammates from London, the boys who were not only able to have the ultimate soccer experience in their backyards, but also have the support system of their friends and family along with it. They seemed to have the best of both worlds.

Sundays were always greeted with open arms by the reserves. After a tough week of training, we'd have a day to sleep in and take a break both physically and mentally. Seb, Ingi, and I made it a habit to go to Miracles, a small coffee shop in Cockfosters, an area near Enfield, to have our traditional English breakfast and take in the Sunday edition of the nation's top tabloids. The tabloids intrigued me. I was used to seeing *The Roanoke Times* on my parents' kitchen table every morning and had occasionally read through *The New York Times* or *The Washington Post* if they were around. The British tabloids were nothing like the traditional papers I was used to. Massive headlines, colourful pictures, and even topless women were splashed methodically throughout the papers, and the news was oftentimes sensationalised.

Many of the tabloids followed a particular pattern: the world's biggest headline on the front page, a photo of a topless girl on page three (the girls were fittingly referred to as "Page 3 Girls"), the rest of the news and betting odds stuffed in the middle, and finally the sporting news on the back. The biggest football story was always plastered across the back cover, complete with picture and more often than not a clever headline. (During my trial Juan Sebastian Veron had scored a good goal for Manchester United, and the headline on the back read "Juan Hell of a Goal".)

Even the sport's section differed in the newspapers. No longer would I see stories discussing Virginia Tech's football team, the Washington Redskins, and everything else in between. Instead, football stories complete with scores and player ratings from England's top five divisions littered the section, followed by rugby, cricket, and Formula One news.

As a player, the newspapers made for either great reading or horrendous reading. The journalists were always the first to bestow their kind words and generous headlines if a player had a great game. Conversely, if a player had a game to forget, I can guarantee they'd want to stay as far away from the papers as possible. The matches were always reviewed thoroughly in the papers, with scores from one to ten issued to each player. Most players would earn between a five and seven. The occasional eights, nines, and even tens were given out to those players who changed the game or had a massive influence. If a player had a game to forget, they'd probably get below five and would not read the papers to find out about it. I remember reading one article where the journalist gave a player a "One" rating and stated, "His best move of the game was walking off the pitch when he was subbed." Ouch.

Although they were somewhat outlandish and not always completely accurate, I noticed the tabloids were a massive part of English culture. They made reading the news simple and appealing. Whenever I boarded the Underground, London's subway system, I'd always see a paper left on a seat, calmly waiting for a new reader to peruse it.

I soon found out that my time away from the pitch, though extremely welcome and often embraced, could often be the hardest part of life abroad. I had to learn how to deal with setbacks on my own. Conflicts that had generally been external up to that point in my life seemed to become internal conflicts as well. I'd always been the best at whatever I'd done. School was challenging but I knew that by putting in the work I'd get good grades. So I put in the work. I was athletic and took new information on easily. It took two years as a baseball player for me to make All-Stars. I wanted it, so I put in the work and got it. With soccer, I'd always been a step ahead of my teammates. For me, it was not surprising. I practised daily and had confidence instilled in me that came from doing so. My mentality was that of a winner. *I'm better at this than you. I've worked harder than you. I practise hard and play even harder.*

Back home, if I had a bad game, I'd erase it from my memory and look forward to the next one. It was just a blip in the radar, a low point that I'd fix the following weekend with hard work throughout the week. Things seemed different in my first year at Arsenal, and that external conflict started taking a toll on me mentally. I struggled to erase bad performances from my mind and, boy, were there some bad performances. To further highlight my shortcomings, the coaching staff was no longer babying me, something I'd become somewhat accustomed to as a top player back home. Coaching points were drilled into me. Profanity was tossed around from player to player and from coach to player. Should it have been any different, though? I doubt it. The coaching staff was being paid to produce the best players possible for Arsenal's first team. The players were being paid to perform for that same club. If a player wasn't performing the way he was expected to, the extensive scouting network in place throughout the world could and would line up his replacement.

These thoughts and more all poured through me. Sometimes I'd call my parents with an incredible amount of doubt resonating through the phone line. *Am I really good enough to be here? Was this really the right choice?* It was as if my dad had been prepped for all of this. His anecdotes about setbacks, fighting through them, and coming out on top were so basic. It sounded as if he was expecting my calls and knew exactly what needed to be said. "These aren't just good experiences for your soccer career, Danny. In life you will face adversity regardless what your line of work is. How you respond to it is what will define you."

I was determined to succeed. I did my best to take the coaching points that were being yelled my way as positively as I could. I was convinced that Eddie, the reserve team (or rezzies as they were known) manager, had a personal grudge against me. It was actually quite confusing. His warm smile and personality echoed throughout the hallways of the training ground, but when we were on the pitch it was different story.

One particular day after a Tuesday training session, Eddie asked me what I was doing the following day. Thinking he was simply delving into my personal life, I told him I'd probably spend the day relaxing at home. His response caught me off guard. "I'd like for you to come in – 10.15 for 10.30." *Well, there goes my day off.*

I was pissed off, but did my best to brush it aside. I knew Seb, Ingi, and the other reserves were off, but maybe there'd be a group of players training, some coming back from injury, and some first teamers who needed a session. When I reported to training that Wednesday morning, the training ground was essentially empty. I pushed open the dressing room doors, and there, neatly folded in front of my locker, my kit rested peacefully on its own. I changed, put my boots on, and walked to the double doors that led to the pitches. Looking out towards the pitches, I saw Eddie, four mannequins strategically placed in a pattern, and a bag of balls. I was yet to see another player – first team, reserve, or academy, but figured I'd head to the pitches to avoid being late regardless.

When I approached Eddie, he smiled, asked me how I was, then took me on a jog to get warm. I was still confused. *Where the hell is everybody else? Surely I'm not the only player here.* That day, Eddie had me work on my positioning as a left-back and my distribution. He'd ping a ball at me, forcing me to take a good first touch, call out a mannequin, then expect me to hit it with a flighted ball. After about an hour and nearly two-hundred reps, he told me I was free to go.

Nobody else trained that day, and I know I must have looked like a little brat on the pitch, embarrassed to be the only player training on a day off. My view of Eddie didn't change. I was clearly too naïve at the time to realise that Eddie really did want me to succeed. He'd brought me in that day because he thought I had a chance – a real chance at succeeding in the best league in the world. My mentality started to change slightly. I was clearly in the wrong if Eddie was hammering a coaching point at me. He was doing his job, and I needed to do mine. I wasn't used to it. The only person who had yelled at me the way Eddie had was my dad. Soon I started taking the criticism and correction as positively as I could and was getting yelled at less and less. Though no one could replace my dad, Eddie had slotted into his role as my coach, which meant I wanted nothing more than to impress him. As I began to get more and more comfortable and, more importantly, mentally tougher, I started enjoying Eddie's sessions and was no longer afraid of being yelled at.

Early into my second year at Arsenal, Eddie pulled the reserves aside to tell us that he would be joining Blackburn's coaching staff to work under Mark Hughes. I never thought his departure would be as emotional as it turned out to be. Even Eddie appeared to choke up a bit telling us the news. He'd certainly made an impression on me. As my first professional coach, Eddie had taught me so much. I was not only a far better player than I was in my first year, but I was no longer a mental midget. At times he'd made me feel as if he was singling me out and that I was worthless as a player. It wasn't until he was telling us that he was leaving that I realised how much I'd matured and how I owed that to him. He'd been grooming the group to become professionals. He was preparing us for life at the top of the world's game – not an easy task by any means.

Several months after I left Arsenal for the Championship, England's second division, I picked up a newspaper at breakfast. One of the headlines simply read "A Premier Talent". I'd just signed for Burnley, Blackburn's biggest rivals, and Eddie had told the press that the club had signed a Premiership quality player in me. I was actually taken aback by the article. The man whom I thought was out to get me the whole time had nothing but the best of intentions for me and seemed to believe in me after all.

It took one year abroad for me to understand what sacrifice really meant. Of course I knew what it meant to give up certain things in order to obtain others – I'd passed on many parties, formals, and other social gatherings in high school in order to practise, play in games, and travel to tournaments. Even though I would have enjoyed being at those parties, I did my best to stay focused and concentrate on the goals that I had written down for myself. Cyrus had indirectly been protective of me during high school, preventing me from going to certain parties or gatherings so that I wouldn't get mixed up with the wrong crowds and substances. It angered me at the time that my brother wouldn't let me go to parties and hang out with some of our friends on the weekends. After arriving in England and realising that I wasn't concerned with always going out, I began to appreciate the discipline that my brother had instilled in me and became very grateful.

I began to think more and more about sacrifice when all my friends went off to college. There's a certain routine that students in the United States follow with college coming after high school, and I'd ventured off the beaten path. Every weekend I was showered with pictures and stories from my friends. They didn't seem to have a problem adjusting to their new lives away from home. In fact, they seemed to be having a great time – some probably too good a time. It was tough for me to deal with because I was struggling to adapt to my new life, a life I had chosen. Friday nights for me didn't mean going out to party. Friday meant getting to bed early so I'd be fresh for the following day's training. If we had a game on Monday, then going out on Saturday really wasn't a good idea either, and Seb, Ingi, and I would get a meal and relax around our flats.

I did my best to ignore all the distractions from across the pond, especially when I heard about former teammates of mine who were starring for their college teams while I had seemingly forgotten how to control and pass a ball. *This is living the dream?* I had to keep focused, though. The fact that I could see the end product every day at the training ground helped me want it more. The end product was a spot in the first team's dressing room. Kids all around the world would have given a limb to play in front of an Arsenal scout. I'd been lucky to have that chance. Moreover, I had been offered a contract and had spent a year trying to figure out my football and personal life abroad. Going into my second year, I was mentally and physically stronger. I had one year left to prove to myself that I deserved to be there. The sacrifices I'd made would soon be worth it.

13. Make or break

Before I knew it, July 4th had rolled around again, which marked my return to England. The break had given me so much energy both physically and mentally, and I was raring to get back into training. My first season had been such a massive learning curve for me, and I knew the second year of my contract would be the make-or-break season in terms of getting a new deal at Arsenal or looking elsewhere for employment.

Once again pre-season was jam-packed with double sessions and hours of hard work. I was injury-free, playing left-back, and thoroughly enjoying myself. The first team's first pre-season friendly against Barnet was scheduled for July 17th, 2004, and I was named in the starting eleven along with Manuel Almunia, Lauren, Ray Parlour, Philippe Senderos, Pascal Cygan, Cesc Fabregas, Jermaine Pennant, Dennis Bergkamp, Jose Reyes, and Robin van Persie. I was somewhat nervous to be playing alongside such an intimidating cast of players. Pat Rice, the first team assistant coach, must have noticed me pacing around the dressing room because he slapped me on the back and said, "Relax! It's just a friendly. Go out there and play football." I did just that and enjoyed every minute of the packed Underhill Stadium at Barnet.

Very early in the game our defence was caught flat-footed, and Barnet managed to take a one-nil lead. The Barnet fans went crazy as their team took the lead over the previous year's Premiership Champions. Their celebrations quickly ended, however, when Jose Reyes scored in the 19th and 21st minutes. Robin Van Persie then got on the board in the 29th, followed by Reyes again for his hat trick in the 42nd before Dennis Bergkamp finished the scoring for the first half in the 44th minute to make it 5-1. Bergkamp scored another in the second half, and Francis Jeffers came on as a sub and scored a ten minute hat-trick. The scoring finally came to a close when Quincy Owusu-Abeyie scored the game's final goal in the 70th minute. Despite having gone down a goal early in the game, we left the stadium as 10-1 winners, and the entire Arsenal fan base that was in attendance couldn't help but be excited about the year ahead.

The 2004-2005 season started very positively for me. Ashley Cole's extended holiday due to the European Championships in Greece that summer had given me the chance to train and play with the first team in pre-season. On top of that, I had retained my starting left-back spot in the reserves and even scored my first goal for the club in our opening game of the season, a comprehensive 5-0 away win against West Ham United. I went on to start and play in six out of the next seven reserve team fixtures, only finding myself on the bench when Gael Clichy, Sol Campbell, Mathieu Flamini, Robin van Persie, Jermaine Pennant, and Philippe Senderos all featured against Coventry City in the third game of the season.

I was called into training with the first team quite often due to injuries and took advantage of every second I spent with the club's top players. I began to feel more and more comfortable in training and was no longer intimidated about having to mark some of the most famous players in the world. Even after training had ended I'd usually stay behind and work on my long balls or shooting. After one particular session, I ended up being the last man standing with Jens Lehmann and Gerry Payton, the goalkeeping coach. I loved shooting on Jens because he'd always scream "Harder!" no matter how hard I hit a shot, and I was more than happy to follow his directions. After scoring several shots from outside the box, Jens told me he would pay me £100 if I scored on him with the next shot. With nothing to lose and determined to make him eat his words, I took a touch and fired a low right-footed shot into the net. Jens got up, punted the ball away, and simply said "double or nothing." I obliged and basically repeated what I had just done. Gerry smirked and said, "You are going to make him angry!" Jens kept offering double or nothing until he eventually saved one of my efforts and then said he was finished. We both laughed, called it a day, and made our way back to the dressing rooms.

I was happy with the way I was training and enjoyed matchday Mondays much more now that I was taking part in them. The reserves joked around that we were starting our own unbeaten run, going our first ten games like the first team without a loss. What was so incredible about the first team's run, though, was the fact that it was still going from the previous season and wouldn't end until Arsenal travelled to Old Trafford to face Manchester United on October 24th, 2005. A string of unbeaten games that started at the end of the 2002-2003 season continued for the entire 2003-2004 season, and lasted ten games into the 2004-2005 season, finally coming to an end on the magical number of 49 as the Red Devils controversially defeated Arsenal 2-0 after a dubious foul on Wayne Rooney by Sol Campbell led to a penalty. The famous pizza-and-soup-throwing altercation ensued in the tunnel after the game, and, just like that, one game shy of fifty Arsenal's unbeaten run came to an end.

While all the newspapers and television channels were reporting the incident that took place in the tunnel at Old Trafford, Arsenal's first team fringe players, as well as the reserve team players, were looking forward to and getting ready for the Carling Cup 3rd Round tie against Manchester City. The Carling Cup, now the Capital One Cup, is also known as "The League Cup" and features 92 teams in a knockout format. All 20 Premier League (1st tier) teams as well as the teams from the Championship (2nd tier), League 1 (3rd tier), and League 2 (4th tier) are entered into the tournament that roughly starts in September and ends around March. Premiership teams enter the tournament in the 2nd Round, and those teams that qualified for the UEFA Champions League are given byes to the 3rd Round. The Boss has always been known to give younger players opportunities in competitions like the Carling Cup as well as the FA Cup, and the 2004-2005 tournament was no exception.

That week the players likely to be involved in the game all trained together with both the first team and reserve team staff. It was evident through training which team the Boss had selected to play, but the five substitute spots were all up for grabs with roughly fifteen players hoping they would be on the travelling roster. The morning of the 27th of October all the players were expected to report into training wearing their track suits. A list was posted in the reserve team dressing room and those players not on the list would stay behind and train as normal. Having quite possibly one of the longest last names ever, it is usually easy to see where my name is on a list - if it is on there at all. As I approached the wall with the travelling team posted to it, I was ecstatic to see "Karbassiyoon" amongst the sixteen names listed. Seb Larsson was also on the list and we gave each other a congratulatory hug before making our way to the team coach that would take us to Luton airport. Both Seb and I had endured up and down seasons in our first year as reserves, and being able to experience at least one and possibly both of our debuts together was a great feeling.

The Arsenal bus took us to Luton where we boarded a private plane via a private entrance adjacent to the main terminal. Even though there was enough room for each player to have an entire three seat row to himself, Seb and I sat next to each other and just talked about what the upcoming game would be like. We landed in Manchester about thirty minutes after take-off and took another bus to the Lowry Hotel in Manchester's city centre. It was about 2 o'clock by the time we had checked into our rooms, and we were basically meant to rest the whole day. A pre-match meal typical of the meals we ate at the training ground every day was served three hours before the game, and toast was given to us before we made our way to the City of Manchester Stadium about an hour and a half before kick-off.

A police escort consisting of motorcycle cops on either side of the bus, as well as police cars and more motorcycles in front of us and behind us, led us directly under the stadium where we got out and made our way to the dressing room. Because the stadium was brand new and built as a multi-purpose stadium for the city of Manchester, the dressing rooms were relatively big and unlike anything I had been accustomed to in the reserves. As I walked into the room, one of my loftiest dreams came true in the form of seeing my name across the back of an Arsenal shirt hanging from one of the lockers. My boots and shin guards - all players are asked to place boots and shin guards in a large metal box, known as a skip in England, before leaving the training ground to ensure everyone's gear arrives at the stadium - as well as shorts, socks, and track suits were all neatly placed within the locker. Before each game, Arsenal's captain chooses whether or not to wear short or long sleeve shirts. The entire team follows suit, and multiple shirts are found in each locker in case players want to change into a dry shirt at half-time. I was so happy to be there and now just wanted more than anything to come on as a sub and represent Arsenal's first team in a competitive fixture.

14. The shot heard round the world

"Danny! Danny!" The sound of Pat Rice's voice was barely audible as I sprinted up and down the side-line during the second half. I had heard and seen Pat scream down the side-line so many times during the first team matches I had attended at Highbury, and I knew very well what came next. I was full of energy. I had been warming up for nearly thirty minutes, and the sweat that dripped off my face, accompanied by the steam that disappeared into the night sky from my head, were sure-fire signs that I was more than ready.

So this was it: the moment I thought might never come after having such a roller coaster first season was finally upon me. I was moments away from making my debut for one of the world's largest clubs – the Premiership's current leaders. I was about to walk onto the pitch with guys that I had seen play in World Cups. This was completely different from anything I'd ever experienced, and I embraced it all with open arms. No matter how many reserve team games I had played in, it was very obvious that this was on a whole new level. Sure I'd trained with the first team on numerous occasions prior to that night, but the atmosphere at the training ground was a world away from the bright lights, cameras, and vocal fans that epitomise a top end, first team fixture.

"You're replacing Arturo [Lupoli] and filling in as a left-sided midfielder. Now get your gear on and I'll show you your jobs." Pat's voice was oddly comforting. The guy had intimidated me for a long time, and he would still go on to intimidate me in the future, but the words he spoke that night were far from that. The coaching staff was showing their belief and trust in me. They trusted that I could walk out on the big stage and get the job done – for Arsenal Football Club. I was more than up for the challenge. I had worked so hard the previous year and all the current season with very little to show for it, so I was ready for a change.

I hopped up the small steps that led to my seat on the bench where my shin guards and shirt were lying. Stuart Taylor, our backup goalkeeper that night, gave me a pat on the back and wished me luck as I stripped down to my shorts and socks. I jammed my shin guards into place then pulled the Arsenal's trademark red Nike shirt over my head. Talk about a good feeling. I'd played in Arsenal's kit numerous times up to that point, but never before had my name been emblazoned across the back of my shirt. As I made my way back to the Boss and Pat, the rest of the subs shouted words of encouragement.

After showing me what my roles were on both attacking and defensive set pieces, Pat and the Boss wished me luck and guided me to the halfway line. The ball rolled off the pitch for a throw-in, and the fourth official lifted his substitution board into the air. When Arturo finally made it across the pitch, the fourth official whispered, "Go enjoy it" to me before giving me a little nudge and sending me on my way. It was the 82nd minute. I had roughly ten minutes to be the happiest kid on the planet and enjoy the night I'd been dreaming about for so long.

Despite fielding an extremely youthful side, we had taken the lead in the middle of the second half through a fantastically crafted series of passes involving Mathieu Flamini, Arturo Lupoli, and Robin van Persie. If there was ever a goal that embodied what Arsenal's style of play was all about, then van Persie's strike would be it. Kevin Keegan, Manchester City's manager at the time, had fielded a strong team that featured names like Shaun Wright-Phillips, Robbie Fowler, Danny Mills, and Antoine Sibierski. Even their experience was no match for the quick passing and off the ball movement that led to the goal. Robin's goal had quieted the entire stadium except for one small corner behind the goal we were attacking. The 3,000 travelling Arsenal fans went crazy, singing Robin's name in unison and loving every minute of it. The goal had deflated Manchester City, a team that was already in bad form in the League and now losing to a bunch of kids making their debuts.

By the time I crossed the touchline and entered the pitch, the match was wide open. City were pushing forward, desperately searching for an equaliser that just didn't seem to want to materialise. The fact that the game was so open by that point worried me a little. Both teams were mentally tired and neither team was completely organised. Gaps started forming in the midfield and it looked increasingly likely that if another goal were to come, it would develop through a counter-attack. It didn't take long for me to get involved, and I made sure I played as simply as I could the first time I touched the ball. The last thing I wanted to do was kick-start a City attack by losing the ball, so I made sure I settled my nerves by simply keeping possession.

Within five minutes, I was comfortable and thoroughly enjoying myself. After my first couple of touches, I decided that there was no use being scared. I wanted to enjoy it and there was no way I could do that if I was afraid of my surroundings. The ball was round, there was a goal on each end line, there were twenty-two players on the pitch, and I was one of them. The fear was gone. It was a game of football, a game I had played for fifteen years, and I wasn't going to let some silly butterflies in my stomach ruin my high.

The twenty odd thousand City fans were cheering loudly and doing the best they could to motivate their team. Our fans hadn't stopped singing since we scored, and the atmosphere began to get louder and louder. The songs and chanting made communication tough on the pitch, and it was hard to focus on and hear what my teammates were saying.

Defensively, Sebastian Larsson and I found ourselves working together to stop Shaun Wright-Phillips and his quick, mazy runs. I'd seen him play on television for a year and a half and knew he was crafty, but it wasn't until I was trying to stop him that I truly realised how sharp he really was. Run after run he would come at Seb and me, and run after run he would find no joy in his efforts. We knew just how important it was to stop him and we did everything we could to make sure he didn't get to the end line or get a cross into the box.

On the other side of the ball, I found myself battling with City's right-back, Danny Mills. He was everything I expected of an established defender in the Premiership. The guy was mean, and he was definitely not going to let some unknown kid get the better of him. What a test for me, though. Mills had spent the summer of 2002 representing England at the World Cup in South Korea and Japan and numerous years in the top flight of English football. I'd spent the summer of 2002 guest playing for a team in North Carolina and numerous years in the Virginia Club Champions League. I couldn't have cared less. He was expected to get the better of me and not give me an inch of breathing room, which meant I had nothing to lose.

As expected, Mills wasn't a pushover, and he introduced himself to me by raking his studs down my Achilles tendon as we went up for a header together. When chasing a ball down out for a throw-in, he gave me a nudge from behind once we were off the pitch causing me to fall over. I felt as if he was my older brother and I was getting picked on. I wasn't having any of it. I didn't know what I was going to do, but he was completely in charge and something needed to happen.

As the 90th minute approached, the fourth official signalled that several minutes of extra time would be played. We were still winning one-nil, but I was kind of upset that the game was coming to an end. I had been dreaming of that night since I could remember, and the eight minutes that I had played seemed way too short. The game was far from over, though.

In the 92nd minute, Quincy Owusu-Abeyie was set free down our right hand channel by one of van Persie's precise passes. City's Sylvain Distin respected Quincy's pace, sitting back off him and buying time for the rest of their defence to make it down the field. Quincy attempted to get past Distin several times with his speed and trickery but was unable to and ended up turning out of pressure and finding Johan Djourou near the top right-hand corner of the eighteen. Johan, who was just 17 at the time, was making his debut as well and had come on several minutes after I did. He kept things simple, playing a square ball to Cesc who sat comfortably about twenty-five yards from goal. Cesc let the ball roll across his body, opening up the opposite side of the pitch for him. As he began dribbling across the pitch, I began pulling away from the goal and Danny Mills.

I had learned a lot in my year and a half at Arsenal. My first touch had improved drastically, my finishing had become more precise, and my decision-making had undergone a massive makeover for the better. All these aspects, however, revolved around what I was doing with the ball at my feet. Off the ball, I had come to Arsenal as a kindergarten student, and had learned enough to be graduating with a Master's in off the ball movement. Whether or not I could apply any of the information I had learned to game situations was up to me and not the coaches, but it was plain for me to see that Arsenal's pass and move style had become much more comfortable in my game.

Cesc casually strolled across the box with the ball on his right foot and his head held up. Five City players had recovered and were in good defending positions across their box as he attempted to switch the point of attack. There wasn't much space behind the blue shirts and as Cesc made his way towards me, I began moving away from the goal and Danny Mills. I had seen this situation unfold so many times on the training ground. One winger attempts to get past his man on one side, he is stopped by the defence, he plays back out to a midfielder who looks to switch the attack. The timing needed to be perfect. I wanted to get behind Danny Mills, and the best way I knew how was by making my first movement away from the goal.

Four steps. That's all I needed, and on the fourth step, Mills took the bait. I had made enough space between him and myself that if he didn't commit himself, I would have been wide open. As soon as he made his quick movement away from the goal and towards me, it was time to go. I quickly changed direction, going right back where I came from towards the space Mills had left unoccupied. Cesc's pass was perfect. The timing. The weight. A ball that attacking players dream of running on to. Training ground stuff, except it was a game, and instead of playing around mannequins, we were playing around seasoned professionals. One simple pass had eliminated three defenders and the other two were stranded on the other side of the box.

City's defence had gone from five strong plus a goalkeeper to just the goalkeeper. So is the nature at the top level. People ask me all the time what it was like playing with Cesc. That pass defined what it was like. The best players in the world only need one second to completely destroy and dissect their opposition. Cesc was sixteen at the time, and the ball he played was what you'd expect from a seasoned professional.

Before I even touched the ball, Robin had already started his run towards the goal, anticipating a cross or deflected shot that he could easily tap in. I could feel Mills behind me. I let the ball roll across my body then took a touch with the inside of my left foot. I knew I had one chance to take the touch, and if it was good enough, it'd completely cut Mills out of the play. If I took a bad touch, I might only be able to cross the ball or lose it in a scuffle with him. I wasn't going to lose the ball here, though. My touch set me up perfectly, and if Mills was going to commit himself to tackling me, I planned on getting my body in the way and going down for the penalty.

Robin called for the ball, his hand held up in the air. I saw him and probably would have passed to him on any other day. It's not every day that you see Robin van Persie sitting unmarked ten yards out from goal and decide to completely blank him. It was 1-0. It was the 92nd minute. It was my debut for Arsenal Football Club, and the ball was begging to be hammered towards the far post. I complied.

If you have ever been lucky enough to live out one of your dream, then you may know the emotions I felt as I saw the ball sail past Ronald Wattereus and into the net. I never expected to score or even be put in a position where scoring was a possibility. It was like a dream. One of those dreams where everything is going right and you can't believe how or why everything is falling into place, but it is, and for that little bit of time you couldn't care less about anything else in the world. I've had those dreams where I wake up to the disappointment of realising that it was not real and had not really happened. But when I scored that day, there was no waking up. I was already awake and living my dream.

There was one place I could have put the ball in that instance, and I made sure to put it just there. Just as I had done for so many years growing up, I kept my eye on the ball just long enough to see it cross the line before celebrating the goal. The net enveloped the ball as if it had been expecting it, and our travelling fans exploded. I looked to my right to see all our red and white clad fans jumping up and down only twenty yards from me. They'd travelled three and half hours to watch a bunch of teenagers step up to the plate and produce. I'd like to think they weren't disappointed.

Cesc was the first to join me. I basically jumped into his arms. We were both yelling. He just kept screaming, 'Danny!!!' as we hugged, both laughing and smiling. Sebastian joined us next, jumping so high that he nearly cleared both of us. Johann, Robin, Mathieu, Quincy, and Justin Hoyte all ran over as well. We all turned and started walking towards our supporters - one arm around each other, and one arm up in the air. Flashes from cameras went off everywhere. Before making our way back to our half, Seb ran over to me, put his arm around me, and just said, 'you scored!', as if I was completely oblivious as to what exactly was going on. A photographer captured the moment and it is by far my favourite picture of the whole night. Everything is perfect – rain is falling in the background, sweat is all over my hair, and we are both laughing hysterically. There's no way I could have done it by myself. It had taken us several years to get to that night, and we both knew how much hard work we had put in away from all the cameras. The joy in our faces was genuine. We had arrived.

Robbie Fowler scored for Manchester City off a free kick about a minute after I scored, but it was too little too late. The referee blew the final whistle to confirm that we had done it. 2-1 over Manchester City away from home with a bunch of kids. Our confidence was through the roof. The Sky Sports cameramen raided the field and several of them made a bee-line towards Robin and me. Philippe Senderos and Johann walked over to me and sprayed me down with water as television cameras sat one foot away from my face and captured everything. We all gathered to applaud our travelling fans and then made our way back to the tunnel to exit the pitch.

The mood in the dressing was fantastic. The staff was pleased with the way we had played, and we were definitely happy with the game's outcome. The Boss was particularly happy with the win because the first team's previous trip to Manchester had resulted in the end of the amazing unbeaten run. So many people in England had written off the youngsters, but the club had made a statement and a strong one at that: not only were the first team regulars powerful on the pitch, but the new batch of talent coming through the ranks seemed strong enough to hold their own at the top level.

There was no need to hang around Manchester longer than we needed to, so as soon as the Boss was done speaking, we were all to get showered quickly and get back to the team bus. I packed my shirt and shorts in my bag before making my way out of dressing room and couldn't wait to turn on my phone and call home. As soon as the phone got a signal, it started going absolutely crazy. One, two, three...twenty text messages in all. Voicemails poured in too. I guess people had watched. Friends and family from England and the United States had sent congratulatory text messages. Even Steve Rowley texted me asking, "What are you doing scoring?!"

I knew the game hadn't been televised in the United States, but I was sure there were other means of finding out the result. After talking to my parents, I found out that my dad had locked himself in his office, closed the blinds, and listened to the game via internet radio. His employees still laugh when they describe the shriek they heard from his office that day. Kayvon Sarmadi, a good friend of mine, later explained to me that he was watching the Fox Soccer Report on television late that night when he saw me score and basically flipped out. Michael Milazzo, one of my former coaches during my brief spell at CASL, was one of the only people from back home who actually saw the goal live because the hotel he was staying in during a trip to Africa was televising the match.

After finishing up at the City of Manchester Stadium, we headed to the airport and boarded our chartered jet. The Arsenal bus picked us up at Luton airport and brought us back to the training ground to bring an end to an eventful day. As I was walking down the aisle towards the bus's exit, the Boss smiled and said, "Don't dream about your goal too much tonight." Although I always tried to listen to the Boss as much as possible, I was unable to take his advice in this instance and actually watched the game again when I got back to my flat because it was being replayed on Sky Sports.

The following morning, I woke up with a smile on my face, full of energy and ready to train. I was greeted with several congratulations and other kind words from both the staff and the players when I arrived at the training ground. The youth team secretary had put together a collection of the day's tabloids for me to take home. My grin seemed to be printed on the back of every major newspaper in England. The press had obviously been stunned by the result, and the phrase "Bouncebackability" was being thrown around everywhere. Whatever the journalists said, the general consensus was clear throughout England: the future of the red side of North London was bright.

Despite having such a memorable experience the night before, I had only played about ten minutes and hadn't qualified for a warm-down. I joined in with the first team and the congratulations and jokes continued. At one point in the training session, in between drills, Thierry congratulated me and asked about the game. Patrick Vieira came over and jokingly interrupted Thierry by saying, "So Danny, you think football is so easy, don't you? You come on for ten minutes, you score the winner and you are the hero. Football is good, no?!" Football *was* good. I was on a high and couldn't wait for the next game. I had become comfortable with the world's best players, but more importantly I had enjoyed my first taste under the lights. I knew what it was like and what it took to play at the top level. I also knew that I was still miles away from where I wanted to be within the club and my career in general.

15. The kids are alright

Training continued as usual after that memorable night in Manchester, and the confidence I had gained in my brief stint as a first teamer shone brightly in my time with the reserves. I started in the next reserve match at home, a 3-2 win against Watford, where I put in a convincing performance at left-back. I was strong in my tackles, efficient with the ball at my feet, and fearless on the pitch. I didn't approach the game lightly, but I did feel much more comfortable at the Underhill after playing under the bright lights of the City of Manchester stadium.

The Boss, accompanied by the rest of the first team staff, was sure to be at the reserve game in order to keep tabs on the younger players coming through the system. It was nerve-racking coming out of the dressing room and seeing the Boss, Pat Rice, Boro Primorac, and Gerry Peyton all seated in the front row, but it was a great opportunity to show everyone why I belonged with the first team. The first team staff was at nearly every match we played in, and playing well in the reserve team fixtures was the best way to get called in to play with the big boys.

I was extremely pleased that I had done well in the reserves because I knew the left-back spot in the next Carling Cup game was still a toss-up. Sebastian was doing very well in the reserves, but the back-line was clearly not his best place on the pitch. He needed to be in the midfield, where he could use his deadly accurate right foot to get crosses in the box and play strikers and other midfielders in behind the opposing back four. He hadn't done badly against Manchester City, but my confidence and game against Watford helped show the Boss that I was up for the challenge and ready to step in against Everton.

The day before the game was exactly as it had been before the City game. The pool of players, about twenty-two of us in total, who had a chance to make the squad that would face Everton were all in training with the first team staff on the first team pitches. I knew we would be setting up in the starting eleven to work on team shape and set pieces, so I couldn't wait to get through the warm-up. We took our light jog with Pat Rice, partnered up and worked on technique, and finished off with four and five versus twos.

The Boss called us all in. His French accent was evident as he explained that since we had done such a good job against City, he wasn't going to bring in many of the older players. Edu looked as if he would be replacing Cesc, and Pascal Cygan was nowhere to be seen. Two changes, I thought. This is what happens when you are at such a big club with so much quality. All the reserves were counting, and you could see it. There were going to be sixteen uniforms made for the game against Everton, and twenty-two of us were training. Six of us were going to be left out and everyone hoped they were lucky enough to be on the pitch or on the bench. Two weeks before I had wanted nothing more than to be on the list that travelled. This time, however, being on the list wasn't enough. I wanted to be on the pitch from the beginning. The Boss continued, "In yellow I want Almunia, Karbassiyoon, Senderos, Djourou, Hoyte…" That's all I needed to hear. I was going to be starting against Everton at Highbury and I was certainly up for the challenge.

I sure had come a long way from the previous season. It hadn't even been a full year since I had made my reserve team debut, and I was now set to start against a Premiership side that featured such names as Thomas Graveson, Tim Cahill, Marcus Bent, Kevin Kilbane, and Joseph Yobo, among other established pros. These were guys I had read about in the paper every weekend; guys I would watch on Match of the Day on Saturday and Sunday nights. Arsenal's starters that night, however, were on the complete opposite side of the experience spectrum. Nine of the starting eleven players were aged 21 or younger with the only over-age players being Manuel Almunia, who had made his debut against Manchester City several weeks before, and Edu, our Brazilian midfield maestro, who would use his experience to lead and calm a very excited and young Gunners side.

Despite being a home game, our preparation was treated just like the previous game in Manchester. The team met at the training ground around nine in the morning and boarded the coach, which took us to the Four Seasons Hotel in Canary Wharf where we spent the day resting and preparing for the match. Sebastian brought his playstation with him, and we spent most of our time in the room either napping or playing Pro Evolution Soccer. The day was broken up by lunch around noon, followed by tea and toast a couple of hours before the match.

I wasn't terribly nervous during the day and quite enjoyed relaxing at the hotel and concentrating on the game that was to be played in a couple of hours. I knew I could handle the big stage and was excited about getting to play at Highbury in front of our own fans. It wasn't until the pre-match meeting at the hotel that I started to get a bit nervous. While he was addressing the team, the Boss specifically warned me of Tim Cahill's late runs into the box and his aerial dominance once he was in there. I wouldn't really be marking Cahill in free play too much because he generally played more centrally, but his recent form in the League had been frightening, especially from set pieces, and I couldn't wait for the test.

Even though our team that night consisted of players from all over the world, the Boss conducted his team talk in English, as he always did when addressing the team or any group of players. If a new signing or certain player was unable to understand what was said, another player would help translate once the Boss was finished speaking. His speech and demeanour was calm and inspirational, and above all it prepared us all for the big night ahead.

Looking back at the starting line-up and who we had on the bench that night, I can't believe just how young our team actually was. I was barely twenty years old and basically middle-aged. No one on the team thought twice about his age though. We all knew we had what it took to make it at the top level, and the belief that was coursing through our bodies was almost enough to win the match. We were getting the chance to play in front of 28,000 Arsenal fans, the world's greatest manager, and millions of others on television. All the newspapers were writing us off, thinking that what had happened in Manchester a couple of weeks before was surely a fluke, and a repeat against such a strong Everton side would be borderline impossible.

Per the typical first team routine, the bus left the hotel about two hours before kick-off. Even though the police escort was back in action, London traffic during rush hour makes getting anywhere in the city at least an hour long journey, and that night was no exception. As the bus turned down Avenell Road and pulled up to the Marble Halls, I remembered the first time I had seen Highbury with Steve during my trial and couldn't help thinking how far I'd come from then. Instead of getting out of Steve's car on a peaceful Sunday afternoon, I was walking off the coach in my tracksuit on match night at the Home of Football. The bus crept to a stop in front of the Marble Halls, a scene I had witnessed numerous times on the weekends when I would watch the first team play. The coach doors opened and the team filed off one by one. It honestly felt like a red-carpet Hollywood premier. As I made my way off the bus, thousands of people on either side of the steps snapped pictures, waved, and called my name before I disappeared through the massive black doors.

We made our way to the dressing room, a small but historically rich room that had accommodated such players as Ian Wright, Steve Bould, Marc Overmars, Tony Adams, and many others in its recent past. A far cry from the typical NFL locker rooms that boast flat screen televisions, massive lockers, plush carpet, and wireless internet, our dressing room was small, cramped, and perfect. I didn't need to watch television or check my email to get ready for the game. The line-up was written on the board, and all I needed to know was that my ten other teammates were ready to do battle.

As I took my tracksuit off and changed into my warm-up gear, the rumble from the fans already inside the stadium and the noise that seeped through the open windows from the road below excited me. My shirt hung in the corner furthest from the dressing room's entrance and seeing it sent chills down my spine. Long-sleeved, red, and branded with our team's badge – I couldn't wait to pull it over my head and walk out of the tunnel.

The warm-up was both exciting and completely routine for me. Not only had I seen the first team do it so many times at their games, but our warm-ups in the reserves emulated the first team so as to make the transition easier. It was exciting because I knew several good friends of mine were in attendance and seated somewhere in the stadium. Where – I had no idea, but I knew they were there and that's all that mattered. The crowd was very receptive to us when came out of the tunnel, and I heard a lot of fans call my name and tell me how great my goal against City was. Although I had made my debut at City several weeks before, I couldn't wait to play in front of our own fans in our own stadium and see what it was like to have the support of thousands behind us during the game.

The view was different from the pitch but I was comfortable and happy to be where I was. I smiled and waved to my teammates who had been left out of the squad and were sitting in the paddock as I made my way back inside the tunnel. The dressing room was hectic and loud. Pat Rice was pumping players up, especially the defenders, and making sure everyone knew their jobs. All the last minute tape jobs were completed, and soon after the shirts that had been hanging so peacefully on their pegs were taken down and put on.

The Boss gave his final pep talk, a more exciting and energising speech than the one he had delivered in the hotel, and the referees signalled that they were ready for us. Pass and move. Play simple. Respect the opponent. Most of all, enjoy it. I hadn't been nervous in the hotel, but as I left the comfort of the dressing room and hopped down the small steps that led to the tunnel, I felt an entire colony of butterflies manoeuvring erratically in my stomach.

Thomas Graveson walked down the tight corridor, and his Everton teammates followed suit. Marcus Bent stood next to me, his broad shoulders and imposing height making him look like a giant. The tunnel hadn't become any smaller since I had last walked through it, but the fact that there were two rows of eleven players lined up shoulder to shoulder inside it made it seem as if the walls were closing in on me. I couldn't see out into the stadium but I could hear Fatboy Slim's 'Right Here, Right Now' playing through the speakers, and I knew what that meant. The crowd was singing Vieira's song in honour of the captain even though he wasn't playing. Moments later, the announcer introduced us over the music and we began our short walk out onto the pitch.

I walked out of the tunnel and onto one of the most fabled pitches in the history of the game. Lucky me. I could rightfully call this my job, and I wouldn't have traded anything in the world for it. All four stands looked like seas of red and white with the exception of one section of the Clock End where Everton's supporters did their best to encourage their team. I had been to Highbury, or "The Home of Football" as it was commonly referred to, so many times, but never did it feel quite so special to me. The pitch, known to be narrow, was much smaller than I ever thought possible, and the close proximity of the stands to the pitch made it feel as if the supporters were literally on top of the players. It really couldn't have been much better. About a year and half before that night, I was playing for the Roanoke Valley Youth Soccer Association in the Virginia Club Champions League at Berglund Soccer Complex in Vinton, Virginia. And now I was representing Arsenal Football Club against Everton Football Club at Highbury Stadium in North London, England. Things had definitely changed, and there was not a single complaint coming from my end.

More than anything I just wanted the game to get underway so that I could get into the swing of things and forget about how big a night it was for me. I knew I had the rest of my life to think about the players I was playing against and the venue I was playing in. I was still nervous but I knew that as soon as I heard the whistle blow, I'd get comfortable and play the way I needed to.

The game kicked off, and for the first twenty minutes it seemed as if the journalists had been right. We were having a tough time acclimatising ourselves to the pace and strength of our opposition, and our challenges were often mistimed and brash. Eight minutes in, Graveson was presented with a free kick about twenty yards just to the left of the goal. The situation didn't look good at all. The wall set itself up according to Almunia's directions, and we all prepped ourselves for the potential cannon ball that was going to be unleashed by the Dane.

James McFadden ran over the ball first as a dummy before Graveson smacked the ball with his laces and sent it sailing towards the goal. When I turned to see if Manuel had dealt with it, I saw that he was on the ground, sprawled out with a helpless look on his face. The ball rested in the net and the boys in blue went nuts. After leaving Graveson's foot, the ball took a nasty deflection off Pennant's heel and wrong-footed our Spanish keeper. One-nil to Everton after only eight minutes. It certainly wasn't the end of the world, but we definitely didn't expect to be a goal down before the ten-minute mark.

Everton seemed to be out-muscling us, and many thought we didn't have the experience to get the game back under control and put up a fight that was remotely a threat. Individually speaking, I had been welcomed to the game when Graveson went shoulder to shoulder with me, literally sending me crashing off the pitch and into the advertising boards. It felt as if I had run into a large boulder. I made a quick mental note that I needed to get into the gym more often, picked myself up, and got back on the pitch.

An unfortunate injury saw Ryan Smith's game come to an end after only twenty minutes, but his replacement, Quincy Owusu-Abeyie, possessed the tools that we desperately needed going forward. He was fast, strong, tricky, and solely concerned with going forward. Within five minutes of the substitution, one of Quincy's twisting runs had resulted in a fabulous goal, which equalised the game. Pennant had played a perfectly weighted ball into Quincy's path and our Dutch winger used his strength, his power, and his speed to get past two defenders and drive his right-footed effort into the back of the net.

We were back on level ground with the big boys and full of confidence. Suddenly the kids were playing with a purpose again, and the momentum had shifted greatly in our favour.

Edu was absolute class in the midfield and helped control the tempo of the game. Whenever I found myself under pressure or in a tight situation, I always knew I had him as an option. Even if he was under pressure, I was confident that he could do whatever he wanted with the ball and play out of danger. His left foot could handle any situation, and it was incredible watching him prance around the midfield as if he was in training.

With the help of Edu and the other ten Arsenal players that were on the pitch, the half ended at one apiece, and our only complaint was that we weren't winning. Quincy's ability and speed opened doors that previously hadn't existed in the game, and Everton was having a very difficult time handling him. The Boss encouraged us to keep playing our own game and more importantly to believe that we could actually win. The game had turned quite physical as tackles started to fly in from all directions. Edu was lucky not to get sent off after one particular challenge, and Everton were quick to show their disapproval. Several scuffles had broken out in the first half, which only made the game that much more intense and exciting.

I took the fifteen-minute break to gather myself and get ready for the next half. I'd completed forty-five minutes and didn't feel out of place out all. The players I was marking were obviously very good, but I had become accustomed to marking Thierry and Dennis Bergkamp in training. I just kept referring back to that simple thought: I was there for a reason. I was being told by Pat Rice to continue everything I was doing. Neil Banfield patted me on the back and said, "Well done, son." Before walking back out of the tunnel, I took several sugar pills from the physio to restore some energy and switched my shirt for a dry one.

If we had tried to match the Toffees physically, we probably would have ended up as the losing side. Instead, we started the second half right where we had left off in the first half. Fluid passing and movement on and off the ball created numerous opportunities in front of goal. The home fans soon became very vocal, cheering on their youngsters and providing an atmosphere that made communicating on the pitch very difficult. I literally had to scream at Philippe in order to be heard whenever I was passing a runner on or simply giving directions.

Quincy's prowess in the middle and final thirds of the pitch really began taking a toll on Everton's back four. They were forced to foul him numerous times, if they could catch him, and by no means was he ready to take his foot off the pedal. Unfortunately for me and the other three players in our back-line, the same couldn't be said defensively. Every time Quincy made a dashing run forward, the entire left side of the midfield would be left unoccupied and Steve Watson would have acres of space to play with. I was presented with numerous one v one situations and cherished the challenges. Watson wasn't incredibly quick, but he was crafty and tidy, which at times made him even more dangerous. I didn't give him an inch of breathing room, though. Every time he came at me, I'd keep my eye on the ball and make myself impossible to get around. He managed to get one cross off in the first half, but was rendered useless after that. Very early in the second half David Moyes, Everton's manager, replaced Watson with Leon Osman, a smaller, quicker winger who was also known to be tricky. One down, one to go, I thought. My new job was to make sure Osman didn't feel at all comfortable coming anywhere close to me. I complied happily. I was tackling hard, winning headers, and getting forward at every opportunity.

Within seven minutes of the start of the second half, another one of Quincy's runs resulted in a goal. After beating several defenders, Quincy slipped the ball into the path of Robin van Persie, who played a square ball to Arturo Lupoli. Lupoli didn't need more than a second to embrace the opportunity, and with his first touch he eased us into the lead from six yards out. The stadium erupted, and the sense of belief the manager had put in our minds at the break become more and more apparent.

Defensively, Senderos, Djourou, Hoyte, and I couldn't afford a mental lapse for a split second. Everton continued to attack and we continued to quell their efforts in front of goal. One break in particular led to a lofted cross from our right side that cleared Almunia comfortably and was headed to the back post. I was the only one who had recovered in time, and as I checked my shoulder to see if I was clear for a free header, I saw Joseph Yobo, a six-foot-one Nigerian international, barrelling my way. He had all the momentum in the world and I had to jump from a more stationary position, but I managed to get my head on the ball and direct it over the bar for a corner. Yobo managed to get his entire body on mine and sent me sailing into the net. Manuel and Philippe came over, picked me up, and commended me for my efforts. It was obvious that there was no way we'd accept anything other than a win now. Five minutes from the end, Arturo scored nearly an exact replica of his first goal to put the nail in the coffin. Everyone sprinted to the corner flag and slid into a massive pile as the Highbury faithful exploded into song.

When the referee blew the whistle to signal the end of the game, a sense of relief took over my body. Even though I had played against Manchester City, it had been for a very brief time, and the game was so open when I came on that it made for a very hectic experience. Knowing that I had just completed ninety minutes against one of the better clubs in the Premiership and had come out with a win was an incredible feeling. Not only had I done my job defensively against seasoned professionals, but, more importantly, the team had accomplished what we had set out to do ninety minutes earlier. We fought when we needed to fight and played fantastic football when it was needed.

After the game, as Seb and I made our way to the player's parking lot in the stadium, my phone rang and I answered it. Bob McNab, Arsenal's former left-back and one of my coaches from ESP camp, was on the other end and was calling to congratulate me on my Highbury debut. Along with Paul Mariner and Steve Rowley, Bob had been instrumental in helping me get over to Arsenal, and I was especially proud to be speaking to him after the game. Once I was off the phone, Seb and I drove back to our flats where I watched the game's highlights on television before calling it a night.

16. The Theatre of Dreams

The general mood and atmosphere around the training ground after our comeback win against Everton was awesome. The younger players who had only just played their second game with the first team were buzzing with confidence, and training was noticeably more intense. As we continued to progress in the Carling Cup, nothing was guaranteed for any of the players, and spots were available to be taken in the starting eleven as well as on the bench. Our two wins meant we had made it to the final eight of the competition, and several days after our triumph at Highbury, the quarter-final draw was made on Sky Sports. Training had already ended for the day, and all the televisions at the training ground were tuned in to see what we'd be facing in the next round. The draw was done in a very similar way to someone picking the winning lottery numbers, so when the host plunged his hand into the machine with the eight balls in it, a sense of excitement drew everyone closer to the screens.

Watford were the first team that the host drew with Portsmouth coming out next, making the first match-up one of the less exciting battles of the quarter-finals. Fulham were then informed they would be hosting Chelsea in a southwest London derby that was sure to be entertaining. That left four teams in the machine: Tottenham, Liverpool, Manchester United, and us. The excitement levels rose at the training ground when Tottenham were pulled out of the machine because, if we were selected next, it would mean we would be travelling to White Hart Lane to face Spurs in a massive North London derby. The host drew Liverpool next, however, which meant the inevitable for both Manchester United and us. With only two balls left to choose from, Manchester United's ball was selected first, which meant we would be travelling to Manchester for the second time in the competition.

So that was it. We'd be facing Manchester United at Old Trafford in the quarter-finals of the 2004-2005 Carling Cup, and I'm not sure that I could have been more excited. I had dreamed of playing in massive games like this for so long. I remember spending countless days in my backyard, scoring game winners in games that I had completely made up in my imagination. This was different, though. This was real, and the excitement that accompanied the match was unlike anything I'd ever experienced. It wasn't only the idea of getting to play against Manchester United at Old Trafford that made the game so special. No. It was the fact that I'd be representing Arsenal Football Club against Manchester United. Although I had only been in England for a year and a half, I knew just how big a game it was when the Gunners and Red Devils met. Millions of fans from around the world were sure to tune into the match, and it was scheduled to be played at prime time on a Wednesday night on Sky Sports 1 in the United Kingdom.

In the weeks leading up to the game, the staff around the training ground kept us updated as to how many tickets had been sold. The number started at 30,000 the first week, with Arsenal's allotment completely selling out as soon as they went on sale. Within days, the number had jumped to 40,000 then 50,000 and finally 68,000 - the stadium's maximum capacity. Advertisements for the game started being shown on television soon after, and in one particular commercial my goal against City was shown. I couldn't wait for game day and jokingly hoped that Manchester was 'my city' and that another game winner was in store for me.

I was third in the pecking order at left-back, behind Ashley Cole and Gael Clichy, but I knew the Boss would choose a young side again to travel back up to Manchester. With that said, Gael was a year younger than me and was still making a name for himself in the first team. Gael had been injured for the first two games of the Carling Cup, which gave both Sebastian Larsson and me an opportunity to play in the left-back spot. I couldn't help but wonder what my chances were at Arsenal with Gael there. From the first day that I saw him at pre-season in 2003, I could tell he was going to be an international superstar. Even at just 17, he was strong, quick, and incredibly feisty. When he made his debut with the first team against Rotherham in the Carling Cup the previous year, he looked as if he had been playing in the first team for years.

Once again I was named in the travelling squad, and our day was exactly the same as it had been when we played Manchester City several weeks earlier. Instead of driving to the City of Manchester Stadium from our hotel, however, we headed towards Salford and Manchester United's 68,000 seat Old Trafford stadium. (The capacity of the stadium has since been increased to roughly 77,000.) Aptly nicknamed "The Theatre of Dreams", Old Trafford resembled a fortress as the bus pulled up to the players' entrance. When we got off the bus, truckloads of abuse were hurled our way from United fans and cheers came from our travelling fans. The visiting team dressing room was much smaller than I had expected, and it was very cramped once everyone was inside.

I took my seat where my shirt hung on its peg and picked up the copy of the matchday programme that rested on top of my kit. As usual we'd arrived with plenty of time before kick-off, so most of the guys took ten minutes to look through the programme and see what United's outlook on the game was. Shortly after, everyone began replacing their track suits with their game kit, and it was time to warm up.

It wasn't until I finally walked out of the tunnel for warm-ups that I noticed how big and intimidating the stadium actually was. The pitch wasn't in the best of conditions and was actually very slippery. Many people were still filing into the stadium, but the atmosphere was already electric. Our fans were making noise, and I knew we'd need all the support we could get from them to make it through the next ninety minutes.

The Boss' pre-match speech was similar to the two speeches he had given in the matches that I had been a part of earlier in the competition. Although we were about to go out and take on Manchester United in front of their home crowd, we had an air of confidence about us that was much more obvious than in the previous matches. A month and a half earlier, many of us had no idea what to expect when we set foot on the pitch against Manchester City. We had grown a huge sense of belief in our ability over the course of several weeks, and victories over Manchester City and Everton, who were in third place in the Premiership when they made their early exit in the Carling Cup, gave us the confidence we needed in the upcoming match. We definitely respected our opponents, but we didn't see anything as impossible and truly believed we could walk out of the tunnel at Old Trafford and leave as winners once the final whistle was blown.

The press assumed both teams weren't going to field full strength teams, and they weren't wrong. Our back four remained the same as the Everton match apart from Gael Clichy replacing me at left-back. The midfield featured two quick and tricky wingers in Quincy Owusu-Abeyie and Jermaine Pennant and a hardworking core in Mathieu Flamini and Sebastian Larsson. Robin Van Persie and Arturo Lupoli would attempt to provide us with a cutting edge up front. Manchester United's squad featured eight full international players, including Tim Howard, John O'Shea, Phil Neville, Wes Brown, and Eric Djemba-Djemba.

By the time the referees came to knock on our dressing room door, everybody on the team was ready for war. The physios finished up all their pre-match massages and wrap jobs, and all the starters made their way towards the tunnel. I picked up my huge bench jacket and filed out of the dressing room with the rest of the substitutes. The tunnel was very different from Highbury's: the ceiling was high and there was probably enough room for a car to drive into it. It wasn't nearly as intimate as our home ground's tunnel, but it was unique in its own way.

The United players soon appeared from their dressing room and walked past us without saying a word. I couldn't see the pitch from where I was standing, but the noise reverberating into the tunnel was deafening. The Sky Sports cameramen stood facing the captains with their backs to the pitch. When the stadium's announcer gave the signal, the crowd managed to get even louder, and we began our short walk towards the pitch.

Although most of the tunnels in soccer stadiums are located at the halfway line, Old Trafford's is located in one of the ground's corners. As soon as all the starters made their way onto the pitch and were presented to the crowd, the rest of us began our short walk along the side-line to our bench. Frank Simek and I climbed the stairs to our seats and sat down next to each other. The view was incredible. Of course, the view would have been one million times better if I had been on the left side of our defensive half waiting for the kick-off, but settling for a spot on the bench in one of the world's biggest rivalries wasn't a terrible consolation.

The referee's whistle was barely audible over the excited crowd. The Boss was still making his way to the bench as the game got underway. Just seconds after United kicked off, we won the ball and Justin Hoyte composed himself in possession at right back. He opted for the safe option and played another backward pass towards Johan Djourou, who was playing as our right-sided centre-back. We didn't want to rush anything and certainly wanted to keep the ball in order to establish some sort of control on the game away from home. Our plan immediately went wrong. As Johan waited to control the routine ball played back to him, he lost his footing and failed to make any contact with the ball. Philippe saw the danger immediately and started running towards our goal, but it was already too late. Right off the kick-off, David Bellion had started chasing the ball in order to apply pressure on our back four. When Johan lost his footing for a split second, Bellion took full advantage of the situation and collected the ball at his feet. He took one touch and then another. Philippe contained the danger momentarily before Bellion cut sharply inside on his right foot. Gael came storming across the top of the box to provide cover but also slipped, giving Bellion a clean look at goal. His effort went zipping towards Almunia and managed to skip just under him, slamming into the back of the net moments later.

Absolute pandemonium took over the stadium. It had only taken twenty seconds for United to score, and the supporters went absolutely mental. I couldn't believe it. The scoreboard hadn't even reached one minute yet. Our manager was just about to sit down in his seat, and we were already down a goal. What a nightmare. All I could hear was 65,000 United fans shouting, "United! United! United!" The fans seated behind us were laughing and calling us names. Conceding a goal in the first minute of any game is tough to deal with, but conceding a goal in the first minute to Manchester United at home was the last thing we wanted to happen. I knew we'd have to dig really deep to come out on top now.

Even though neither club had put out their top eleven players, the game was still very heated and proved to be a battle throughout. United, with the crowd behind them and that early goal, proved to be the better side. They weren't too concerned with attacking and only went forward if they needed to. As long as they defended well and kept a reasonable amount of possession, the game was theirs. We also tried to maintain possession and tried to create chances by catching their defence out of position when we had the ball. Unfortunately we were able to put together very little, and our best effort, a Jermaine Pennant curling free kick, was palmed away easily by Tim Howard.

Several minutes after the scoreboard hit forty-five minutes, the referee blew his whistle to signal half-time. The team needed the short break. Not from the physical aspect of the game, but more so from a tactical aspect. It was mentally draining to go down a goal after twenty seconds, and our team was so young that many were struggling to change the way we approached the situation. The Boss obviously wasn't happy with the score, but dwelling on such an early goal was pointless. We had forty-five more minutes to get at least one goal. Johan was clearly upset, but the only words coming from the team were words of encouragement. Not one person would have dared to call him out. Even though he was seventeen and from Switzerland, he knew how big a game it was and didn't need to be reminded. It could have happened to anybody, and the team was fully aware of that.

As soon as the second half started, I was dying to get on the pitch. I wanted to contribute to our performance and was confident I'd do just fine when I came on. More than anything, though, I wanted to score again. I wanted to grab the equaliser and quiet United's support. Unfortunately for us, the second half picked up right where the first half left off. United continued to stop us stringing any passes together and prevented us from being any sort of threat. Tempers began to flare and the challenges began getting slightly dirtier. A short bust-up featuring Hoyte, Robin, and Kieran Richardson resulted in several yellow cards being issued.

I was told to start warming up early in the second half and spent a majority of the final forty-five minutes stretching and running up and down the side-line. Both Gerard Pique and Guiseppe Rossi, who now play for FC Barcelona and Fiorentina respectively, were warming up next to me and smiling as their fans asked for waves and screamed words of encouragement their way. The treatment I received differed slightly. One fan in particular thought it would be funny to call me a "wanker" every time I ran past him while he used his hands to motion what he thought of me. I ignored them all to the best of my ability and concentrated on getting myself ready in case I was called on. With about fifteen minutes left in the half, I heard Pat Rice's familiar voice screaming my name down the side-line. It was time to see what this rivalry was all about.

Pat told me I was taking Gael off and going on as left-back. The staff wanted me to get forward as much as I could and almost play as a wing-back because of the score.

I was happy with that. I would have been happy going on as a goalkeeper, to be completely honest, but I wanted to be near the United goal as much as I could and was content knowing I had permission to attack whenever possible. I quickly looked over my jobs, swapped my warm-up shirt for my blue Arsenal shirt, and made one more stop before heading to the halfway line. The Boss put his arm around me, briefly smiled, and said, "Go and score again."

As I waited for a dead ball situation so the substitution could take place, I took a minute to look around the stadium and tried my best to take a mental snapshot. The sky was pitch black. The floodlights were blinding. The noise from the crowd was enchanting, and the smell of grass filled the air. The only word that could be used to describe the situation was *daunting*. I didn't have butterflies anymore. It was beyond that. I was standing at the halfway line of one of the most renowned stadiums in the world, fully aware that an enormous majority of the crowd wanted to see me fail miserably.

The ball rolled off the pitch for a goal kick about thirty seconds later, and Gael acknowledged our fans before making his way off the pitch. As he jogged towards me, I heard a loud, distinct cheer echoing from all four sides of the stadium. The words, "Who the f******* hell are you?" were being shouted, and they soon developed into, "Who the f***, who the f***, who the f******* hell are you?"

"Who am I," I thought? "Who am I? I'm Danny. I'm the guy that knocked your cross-town rivals out of this competition. Who exactly are you guys?" I laughed at myself.

Never had so many people paid me so much attention. Too bad they all hated me. The song grew louder and louder and continued as I sprinted across the pitch to get into position.

Just like my debut, the game was very open when I came on, and we were pushing as many numbers up as possible, desperately seeking the equaliser. We had been up a goal when I came on against City, and our main objective was to kill the last ten minutes of the game. Now that we were down a goal, everything we did was aimed towards getting the ball in the back of the net, and that sometimes left us exposed at the back. There was a massive hole in the midfield, and United countered often, bringing the best out of our back four.

I didn't see too much of the ball because of our very direct manner of play, but I was active defensively and enjoying every tackle I made. Bellion managed to break free down my side at one point, and the stadium responded with a roar. He kept chopping in and out, trying to turn me one way and then the other. I kept retreating and waiting for the right moment to commit myself, when suddenly I felt the earth give from beneath me. My stud had slipped right across the wet surface and I went crashing down towards the pitch just as Johan had done in the first half. It all happened very quickly, and I was back on my feet within a second, but I knew Bellion had passed me and was on his way towards our goal. When I looked up, I saw Philippe come flying into the scene with a perfectly-timed tackle. That's what it was like playing at the top. Phil's positioning couldn't have been any better, and as soon as I slipped, he was able to make the play and keep us within one goal.

The final minutes of play were hectic and spent in front of United's goal. No matter how close we came to scoring, the boys in red always managed to send the ball sailing out of the area. I heard a high-pitched beep and looked over to see the referee staring at his watch and pulling his whistle to his mouth. The sound of his whistle and corresponding cheer from the home crowd signalled the end of the game. I was gutted and couldn't believe the series of events that from the first twenty seconds of the game had influenced the outcome. Losing was one thing, but losing to Manchester United hurt even more. The team walked over to and applauded our fans who were still singing loudly. On my way back to the dressing room, I stopped and spoke to Tim Howard. Even though he was technically considered the 'enemy', he was and still is an inspiration to all the young Americans trying to make it in England. Not only had there been two Americans on the field at Old Trafford that night, but Frank had also been on the bench for us, and both Jonathon Spector and Kenny Cooper were on the books at United. Who would have thought that two of the best teams in the world would ever include five American players at any given time?

The dressing room wasn't as lively as it had been after the previous two games. Everyone took their seats and listened to the Boss give us his take on the game. He didn't need to say much. We all knew we hadn't played the way we were capable of playing, but it was no use hearing it over and over. We had to take the positives from the game and the tournament as a whole. Playing against three Premiership teams and recording two wins with a very young group of players was something to be proud of. I was happy to have been lucky enough to play in one of the world's most exciting games for one of the world's most entertaining teams.

After gathering all my belongings and collecting my shirts, I headed to the team bus where the team was greeted with a series of cheers and boos from United and Arsenal fans. We made the short drive back to Manchester airport, boarded our flight, and were back in London several hours after the game had ended, thus completing our Carling Cup run for the 2004-2005 season.

17. From Gunner to Tractor Boy

After getting over the disappointment of being knocked out of the Carling Cup, the reserve team fixtures continued until the short Christmas break given to those players not involved with the first team over the hectic holiday period.

One of the best and most highly anticipated reserve team matches of the season took place right before the week we were allowed to go home. Getting to play against Tottenham was always one of the most intense and fun matches of the season simply because of the amount of hatred between the two clubs. I remember going to watch my first Arsenal-Tottenham derby at Highbury during my first year at Arsenal and seeing the entire stadium surrounded by police on foot, on horses, and on motorcycles. Riot police were also in place in massive riot trucks with metal shields covering the windscreens. The passion and intensity inside the stadium during the match and then outside on the streets after the match is in a league of its own. Because of the two clubs' close proximity in North London, even the reserve team fixtures drew big crowds that made for exciting atmospheres.

Our December 6th match with Tottenham in the reserves was no different, and the game was made even more special when I heard that a large group from Arsenal America, North America's Official Arsenal Fan Club, was in London and at the game to cheer us on. The Underhill was jam-packed full of spectators as we put on a show and ended the game as 2-1 winners. The group from Arsenal America was very vocal and even started singing my name in a song whenever I won a ball or had anything to do with the build-up offensively. I had met several from the fan club at the T-Bird pub, located right by Highbury, before a first team match the year before, so it was nice to see some familiar faces after the Tottenham match.

After showering I met up with everyone who had stayed behind and took pictures and talked to them before getting back on the team coach and heading back to the training ground. Although the only thing I said at the time was probably, "thanks for coming to the game", I was really impressed and grateful that we had fans that were so dedicated.

My flight back home was booked for the 23rd of December, and Brett, my friend who had moved over with me initially, had flown back over to visit and accompany me home.

The day before I was scheduled to fly home Will, my agent, called asking if I was willing to forego my trip home and complete a loan deal to Ipswich Town Football Club. The conversation went as followed:

Will: "Danny, I've got some news you may like. Ipswich Town have inquired about your availability for a one month loan deal that will see you provide defensive cover during the busy holiday period."

Me: "Oh, wow that's pretty great news. When do they want me to come? And am I guaranteed a starting role?"

Will: "Joe Royle (the manager of the club at the time) says you'll be on the bench tomorrow night at home against Wigan. There are a lot of games, though, and he said you'll definitely get your chance. From there it's up to you to keep your spot in the team."

Me: "So, no Christmas in Roanoke?! Where is Ipswich anyway and what do we do from here?"

Will: "I'll ring Joe and have him give you a ring so you can speak to him directly."

Several minutes later I was on the phone with Joe Royle and he was explaining the whole situation Will had presented to me minutes earlier. With several injuries plaguing the team at a critical time, Mr Royle wanted to bolster the Tractor Boys' squad, which currently sat at the top of the Championship (the league below the Premiership). On top of that, the following day's opponents were second in the table, which made for a highly anticipated and crucial top of the table match.

At the time, I didn't really know who Joe Royle was or what he had accomplished in his career as a player or manager. The only thing I did know was that I had politely called him 'sir' several times throughout our conversation, and he kept laughing and saying that he wasn't a 'sir' because he hadn't been knighted yet. After doing a little bit of research online, I found out that Mr Royle had enjoyed a goal-filled career, notably with Everton and Manchester City. He set the record for the youngest player ever to play for Everton when he made his first team debut as a sixteen-year-old, a record that was only recently beaten by James Vaughan in 2005. He was Everton's leading goal scorer for five seasons and also represented England at international level. Once his playing career had come to an end, he made his way into the managing side of the game and had been in charge of Oldham Athletic, Everton, and Manchester City before signing with Ipswich Town in 2002. To be speaking to a man with such a rich history in the game was quite inspiring, especially considering the fact that he wanted me to be a part of his team.

Mr Royle was very easy to speak to, and after roughly fifteen minutes I agreed to the move and was back on the phone with Will. We agreed to meet at Arsenal's training ground the following day so he could drive me to what would be my new home for at least a month.

I can't say it was exactly easy to make the decision to go out on loan, but I knew I had to if I wanted to be serious about my career. The thought of seven days off, especially in the comfort of my own home with my family and friends, was extremely enticing, but the chance to be part of a promotion push with the league leaders of English football's second tier won in the end. Most importantly, however, I would be involved in first team football day in and day out, a commodity that I was unable to enjoy at Arsenal.

The next day I was in Joe Royle's office at Portman Road, Ipswich town's 30,000-seat stadium, signing my one-month loan agreement and meeting the coaching staff. Arsenal would still be paying me my weekly wages, but Ipswich was responsible for my matchday bonuses, which included both appearance and win/draw incentives.

Several hours later, I was pulling the number twelve shirt over my head in preparation for the big night. It's always difficult to walk into a dressing room where you are completely unfamiliar with the surroundings and people, and that night was no exception. I specifically remember Jim Magilton, the captain at the time, seeing me when he walked in and simply saying, "Who the hell are you?" in his thick Northern Irish accent. His serious demeanour had me searching for words, but he soon cracked a smile and introduced himself along with the rest of the team.

Even though I knew absolutely none of my teammates, I could feel just how important a game was about to be played. The mentality in the dressing room and during our warm-up was intense, and it didn't take long for me to realise that our captain had the die-hard attitude of a winner for whom losing was not an option.

The pre-match warm-up and talk were all completed, and, as promised, I was on the bench (probably to the displeasure of the younger boys who were trying to break into the first team). I couldn't believe how welcoming the crowd was when I walked out of the tunnel and made the short fifty-yard walk along the touchline to the bench. All 28,000 seats had been filled for the massive match, and those fans sitting near the touchline called my name out, waving and asking for autographs.

The match ended with us as 2-1 winners, and, although I didn't get on the pitch, I was happy to have the first day under my belt. I knew I'd get my chance because of the sheer number of games and looked forward to representing the Tractor Boys at such an important stage of the season.

We were given the following day off, and I hopped on a train that would take me back to London's Liverpool Street Station. Funnily enough, while I was minding my own business on the train, a boy came up to me and asked me if I could sign his Dennis Bergkamp Arsenal shirt. He was apparently a big Arsenal fan and had recognised me when I boarded the train in Ipswich. After signing his shirt and speaking to him for a short while, our train pulled into London signalling the end of the short trip.

Before I made the short trip to Ipswich with Will I made sure to check out the fixture list for the upcoming matches. The next game, to be played on December 26th, saw us travel to Millwall's new Den Stadium in East London. Boxing Day, as December 26th is known throughout the United Kingdom, is one of the most anticipated days in football in the whole country. Every team plays and the holiday season generally draws in larger crowds. Despite being a national holiday for everyone else in the country,

Boxing Day means business for all the football teams, and that means the matches are treated with the same preparation as any other match in the season. We trained on Christmas morning in Ipswich and were then allowed to go have our Christmas celebrations with our families before meeting back at the training ground that night and taking the bus down to Millwall.

I was allowed to drive back down to London and have dinner there before driving to Millwall to meet the team at the hotel. Sebastian Larsson had been asked to stay over the Christmas period at Arsenal, and his girlfriend and her parents had made the trip over to spend the holidays with him. They served as my family that Christmas, and I enjoyed a Swedish meal fit for kings before heading over to our team hotel in East London.

While I sat in the lobby of our team hotel, I realised I had only been a part of Ipswich Town for a total of three days and was still trying to find a group of players that would help me get assimilated into the rest of the team. I was lucky that the team was made up of a lot of younger players like Ian Westlake, Matt Richards, Dean Bowditch, and Darren Bent, and it was these guys who eventually took me in and made my time at Ipswich much more enjoyable. Unfortunately, the process of integration wasn't immediate, and I found myself partnered with the thirty-year-old Darren Currie as a roommate. Darren had actually signed a permanent deal from Brighton and Hove Albion about a week earlier and was in the same boat as me in terms of meeting people and trying to feel comfortable. He also held the title of Britain's most tattooed footballer at the time and quite frankly scared the hell out of me when we got to our room. It didn't take long for me to realise that he was one of the nicest guys I'd meet in England and a wonderful player as well.

The following day's match preparation was very similar to the preparation I experienced during my first team stint at Arsenal. After our pre-match meal and team talk, we filled the team bus and headed towards The Den. I had heard many stories about Millwall's hooligan firms and die-hard fans, who are known both nationally and worldwide for their reputation as bad boys. The police escort was comforting, but as we approached the stadium, more and more Millwall fans were giving our bus the finger and screaming words that are not really fit for publication. The faces and gestures they made were borderline disturbing, and it was quite shocking to see just how passionate and intense Millwall's fans were about their beloved team. Instead of being greeted by fans who wanted our autographs and pictures when we got off the bus, we were greeted by abuse that was hurled at us from all angles.

The pre-match talk in the locker room was different from the talks I was used to, and Joe Royle couldn't emphasise enough how important each game was now that we were top of the table. Each game, he said, should be "treated like a Cup Final". Just because Millwall were middle of the table didn't mean they would be any easier to beat than Wigan several days before. It didn't take long for me to realise just how competitive the Championship was.

I found my place on the bench and winced as we went 2-0 down after sixty minutes. The Millwall fans started singing, "Premiership? You're having a laugh!" - loving the fact that a middle-of-the-table team was beating the league leaders and potential promotion prospects. Shefki Kuqi, our Finish giant who played up front, got one back for us five minutes later, and I was told to start warming up shortly after. As I jogged up and down the side-line, I heard many of Millwall's fans screaming at me and making fun of me. One particular fan walked down to the advertising boards and started calling my name. I kept ignoring him until he finally said, "My daughter wants an autograph and it's Christmas time. At least give us a look." I turned to see him holding his daughter who was about three or four years old and said I'd give him an autograph after the game. He kept insisting that I wouldn't and that it would only take two seconds for me to do it. After a couple of minutes of me ignoring him and saying, "After the game", I finally gave in and approached him and his daughter. As I got close to him, he turned to the crowd behind him and said, "Do you really think I want your f****** autograph?" Needless to say, the crowd all started laughing and I may have muttered something along the lines of "ha, hilarious" under my breath before finishing up my warm-up and escaping back to the bench.

With five minutes to go, I was told to take off my warm-up gear and was given my instructions in preparation for my Tractor Boys' debut. After being told who I would replace and what I was expected to do on set pieces, I approached the fourth official at the halfway line. Once again, when the Millwall supporters saw my last name on the back of my shirt, the abuse started. "Where the f*** are you from you wanker!?", was probably the most popular question directed my way as I jogged onto the pitch and saw out the last five minutes of the match.

Millwall had scored another goal before I came on, which secured their 3-1 victory and sent us back to Ipswich focusing on our next game two days later against Stoke City at home. Although the result at Millwall hadn't helped our push for the Premiership, I was happy to have made my debut and confident that it wouldn't be long before I was handed my first start.

As promised, the games came thick and fast, and the post-Christmas period saw us play games on the 26th, the 28th, New Year's Day, and the 3rd of January. Luckily Jill, my girlfriend at the time, made the trip across the Atlantic the day we hosted Stoke City on the 28th and kept me company and my spirits high as I adjusted to hotel life in a new town. She even experienced an English footballer's typical New Year's Eve, which was composed of me going to sleep before 12 o'clock simply because we were playing West Ham United the following day.

I really enjoyed the whole matchday experience at Portman Road and relished being involved with the first team on a daily basis. In the Arsenal reserves, I had become accustomed to playing in front of crowds of between four and eight thousand people on a regular basis, but up to as many as 30,000 fans regularly filled the seats at Portman Road. I wasn't really given my first real taste of the Championship, however, until January 3rd, when I was named in the starting eleven for our trip to the south west of England to face Plymouth Argyle.

Even though I was playing in the Championship, an entire league below the Premier League and a world away from all the riches and money of clubs like Arsenal, Manchester United, Liverpool, Chelsea, and Manchester City, I couldn't help but notice how first class everything at Ipswich was. First of all, the training ground was fantastic and very well-maintained. Breakfast and lunch were also served there, which is not the case for many clubs in the lower leagues. The team bus was fitted with a kitchen, plasma TVs, and big leather seats. The pitch at Portman Road has won many awards for being one of the best in England and resembles my living room carpet. Unbeknownst to me, Ipswich had enjoyed a spell in the Premier League several years prior to my arrival and finished high enough to qualify for a spot in the UEFA Cup (now the Europa League), Europe's second most prestigious club competition behind the Champions League. A picture of Ronaldo during his time at Inter Milan challenging an Ipswich Town player hangs proudly from the wall in the cafeteria of the club. I soon figured out why everyone referred to Ipswich Town as a "Premier League club in the Championship".

With that said, it wasn't really a surprise when we boarded a plane to make the trip to Plymouth. It is usually a big luxury for non-Premier League teams to fly, and from the stories I heard from some teammates throughout my career, it wasn't uncommon to make an eight-hour bus ride the day before a game. I had no idea I would be starting, and when the line-up was posted about forty-five minutes before the game, I was very excited to be involved from the first blow of the whistle. The game was very typical of the Championship, a very physical affair characterised by speed and a lot of direct football. Fortunately for me, Ipswich were known to actually play passing football, and we enjoyed quite a bit of possession as we broke down our opposition. I found the first ten minutes tough as I adjusted to the style of play, the speed of the play, and my new teammates. Even though there had been so many games already, we had rarely trained and I was still learning players' names as well as their personal styles of play.

The physical aspect of the game was on another level from anything I'd ever experienced. The difference between each tier of English football is basically the footballing ability and intelligence of the players. As you go further and further down the leagues the football gets sloppier and sloppier, and players begin to rely more and more on their physical strength as opposed to their abilities on and off the ball. This means that the games in the Championship are sometimes almost faster than Premier League games, but more out of control and far more direct. Teams are often said to play "Route 1 Soccer", a phrase that simply implies that a team enjoys playing balls over the top and having their strikers run on to them. Route 1 soccer is usually defined by no build up play, and most of the goals are created from knock downs, sheer speed, and bad clearances.

I was obviously grateful that we kept the ball and attempted building play up from the back, but that didn't necessarily mean that Plymouth, or any other team at that, would approach the game in the same manner. From the left-back position, I had to deal with a lot of aerial balls as well as passes played down my channel. Richard Naylor, or Bam Bam as everyone called him, was playing centre-back alongside me and communicated with me enough to win most of the headers that were played on to me. His timing, tenacity, and strength in the air made him almost impossible to beat aerially. As balls were played in the air, I'd tuck around behind him to provide cover as the other centre-back and right-back tucked in to make a tight three until he could fill back in.

Just before the half, however, one final ball was played onto me that seemed like a routine header. As I positioned myself accordingly, Plymouth's right midfielder was making his approach from the touchline, and the collision that ensued made me feel as if Mike Tyson had just given me a knockout punch that would end my night early. I could have sworn that I had actually made contact with the ball, but apparently the only thing my head made contact with was his head, followed by the ground shortly after. I came to after a couple of minutes to the pungent aroma of smelling salts and was greeted by the team physio and the referee, who made the situation even better by giving me a yellow card. On top of that, the home crowd started booing me as I walked off the pitch to get treatment. I suddenly missed the days of youth soccer when all the parents used to clap when someone who was injured got up and was okay.

I made it back onto the pitch just before the half-time whistle blew and was trying desperately to shake off the blow to my head. When the whistle did blow and we filed into the dressing rooms, the medical staff assessed me again and ran a series of tests to make sure I was alright. I passed the tests and felt aware enough to play. The last thing I wanted to do was come off injured in what may have been the only chance I was given to play at Ipswich. I took the pitch again for the start of the second half and lasted roughly fifteen minutes before being noticeably still "out of it" and making way for Matt Richards. Darren Currie scored twice to secure another three points for us and finally close out the busy holiday schedule. Three wins and two losses left us with nine points out of a potential fifteen and a five-day break before hosting Bolton at home in the FA Cup. Most importantly, however, we were still top of the table and looking to stay there.

The Plymouth trip marked a big step for me both in terms of football as well as socially during my time on loan. I found myself next to Ian Westlake on the flight back home, and after talking to him for a couple of hours we became more than just locker room acquaintances. He was soon inviting me to his house after training, and I was able to spend less and less time in the hotel, which was mentally good for me. Even after I left Ipswich, we continued to speak and made the occasional trip to visit one another.

After taking all three points at Plymouth, it was nice to finally have a little break and have ample time to prepare for the next game. Because of our position in the League table, we were doing everything we could to prioritise, and the next game against Bolton, although important, wasn't a major concern. In fact, if we lost to Bolton, we would have a two-week break at the end of January while the next round of the FA Cup games were being played. That break could prove vital in the final stretch of the season and ultimate push for promotion.

To my delight, I was named in the starting eleven again and only found out when I arrived at the stadium an hour and a half before kick-off. I was especially excited because Jill was still visiting and she rarely got the chance to see me play anymore. The fact that she'd get to see an FA Cup game against Premier League opposition made it even better.

The Football Association Challenge Cup, or FA Cup, is England's largest and most famous tournament. With 762 eligible teams, the tournament begins in August with lower non-professional teams and culminates in May with the final. There are no seeds, so the top teams in the country can potentially face each other very early on. The buzz that accompanies the FA Cup is truly special, especially for lower league teams that are always only ninety minutes away from upsetting some of the best and most famous teams in the world.

I knew it was going to be a tough game, and it was very obvious to see that as both teams lined up in the tunnel. Bolton's squad included names like El Hadji-Diouf, Kevin Nolan, Ricardo Gardner, Ivan Campo, Kevin Davies, and Tal Ben-Haim. Standing next to me was former Real Madrid superstar, five times La Liga winner, and three times UEFA Champions League winner, Fernando Hierro.

Despite having enjoyed the whole tunnel and pre-match experience in previous first team and reserve team games at Arsenal, the sheer excitement and build up to the match never really lost its appeal. Hearing the crowd sing while I waited in the tunnel with 21 other players was probably one of the greatest feelings in the world. Encouraging words from both captains echoed down the short tunnel as every player prepared themselves mentally for the battle ahead. Shortly thereafter, the referees led us out of the tunnel, and we were welcomed by a chorus of cheers from over 20,000 fans.

I enjoyed myself thoroughly in the first forty-five minutes and was playing with the type of confidence that I had enjoyed so much just before signing with Arsenal. Darren Currie and I were linking well down the left channel, and my overlapping runs put me in a handful of crossing situations that were very nearly converted to goals. I was covering a lot of ground and was involved in the attack just as much as I was involved defensively. After twenty minutes' play I mistimed a tackle and forced Kevin Davies off with an injury. His replacement, El Hadji-Diouf, proved to be one of the most mobile and tricky attackers I had faced as a defender. Along with Stelios Giannakopoulos, a recent Euro 2004 winner with Greece, and Ricardo Vaz Tê, a quick and creative Portuguese winger, Diouf and Bolton started creating more and more chances. Defensively, however, we stood our ground and got out of the half without scoring or conceding a goal.

The manager didn't have much to complain about at the half. Not only had we remained a tight-knit unit in the back and midfield, but we were pushing forward and creating quality chances that were begging to be put away. Once again, as the second half got under way, I continued pushing forward and whipping balls into the opposing team's box. I was confident with and without the ball and even drew some loud cheers from the crowd with some quick footwork in tight areas that got me out of trouble.

Unfortunately for us, however, things went sour when Bolton scored three goals between the 60th and 68th minutes. Tommy Miller came on as a sub for us and managed to pull one back, but the damage was done. It was a lesson learned the hard way, and I couldn't believe just how quickly a game could change completely. The difference proved to be Bolton's quality in front of goal, as they finished all three chances they created in that eight-minute span. Had we been able to score one of the chances we made in the first half, the game would have been considerably different. I spent a majority of the latter part of the game working on my one-on-one defending because of how open the game had become. We were still pushing numbers forward looking for a miracle of sorts, and Bolton had no intention of taking their foot off the pedal. I constantly found myself isolated with Diouf, Vaz Tê, and Stelios and managed to not get beaten once.

In the 89th minute, after making a last ditch sliding tackle to prevent Stelios' shot from reaching the goal, the manager replaced me with Matt Richards. Despite having conceded three goals as a team, I was content with the way I had played individually. My competitive edge left me upset with the result, but as I walked off the pitch I noticed the crowd standing and cheering my name. Both Stelios and Diouf shook my hand as I made my way to the bench, and I couldn't believe it. I'd seen Stelios help Greece to

Euro 2004 glory several months before, and Diouf had featured for both Liverpool in the Premiership and Senegal in the World Cup in 2002.

The mood in the dressing room after the match wasn't the worst I'd ever experienced, but it was apparent that the team hated losing and definitely wasn't used to it. The good news was that the loss didn't affect our standing in our fight for promotion and actually gave us a two-week break at the end of January to recharge our batteries. After showering and changing, a club representative came into the dressing room and told me I'd been voted man of the match by one of the sponsors. I followed him to one of the stadium's luxury boxes where I was presented with six bottles of wine in a nice wooden case and met several well-to-do fans.

I met up with Jill in the player's lounge afterwards and said goodbye to the team before we made our way to my car in the gated player's parking lot. Almost every fan in England and the world knows where the player's entrance and exit are, and the fans at Ipswich were no exception. As Jill and I came through the glass doors that led to the parking lot, a couple of thousand fans were lined up behind barriers asking for autographs and pictures. I had exited the same doors and signed a few autographs here and there after previous games at Portman Road, but this time was different. Almost every fan that was behind the barrier wanted a picture or signature, and club security followed me as I walked down the line fulfilling everyone's requests. A couple of the other players laughed at me and jokingly called me "big-time" when they saw the security with me. I loved every minute of it. I always played football because it made me feel happy and allowed me to express myself in ways I never knew possible. The fact that other people also found joy in what I was doing was more than I could have ever asked for.

I think one of the most exciting aspects of playing for Ipswich was the fact that it was a one town team and so very different from London. Having grown up in Roanoke, I was used to smaller towns and found it much easier getting around Ipswich than London. My hotel was ten minutes from the training ground and five minutes from the stadium. I could walk to the town centre, the cinema, and all sorts of restaurants. After match days, depending on whether or not I had played well in the game, I would pick up a couple of papers and read what the press had to say about the team. I found myself in the headline in a couple of papers and enjoyed the pseudo-stardom I was experiencing at Ipswich. Fans soon started recognising me in the streets as well, especially when several members of the team would go to the town centre to walk around and shop after training. It wasn't uncommon for us to take pictures and sign autographs in broad daylight, and it was a unique feeling seeing people point and stare as we walked by.

One of the most interesting things I was introduced to in England took place at the training ground after the Bolton game. One of the many technological advances that the sport of football has benefited from is a company called Pro-Zone. If a team opts to pay to use Pro-Zone for the season, cameras are set up around the stadium which break the pitch down into squares that make up a grid. The entire game can be watched as a computer animation where the players are represented by dots, and it's very easy to see how players may not have stepped together from the back or were too disconnected during a series of plays. On top of that, if your coach says, "Danny, you didn't run much this weekend," you really can't come back with anything because a player by player list is printed of how far you ran, how many sprints you completed, how long you walked for, and a slew of other statistics that can be quite humbling. These statistics can also work in your favour too, of course. For example, if a player generally runs six miles a game and has two games where his performance is far below that, it may mean that the player is tired and needs to let his body rest. In these instances, the player may be told to take several days off training to recover. There is no hiding from the cameras.

After two or three weeks at my new club, I was very happy and comfortable with my situation. I had gone out on loan to improve as a player and most importantly to get as much first team experience as possible. Although I ultimately wanted to go back to Arsenal and fight for my place in the first team, I had to be realistic about my chances of getting past Gael Clichy and Ashley Cole, and I soon started thinking that staying at Ipswich Town might not be a bad thing at all. I was getting along with my teammates and was happy with everything Ipswich had to offer. Nike had also taken notice of my recent success, and they offered me a contract as soon as my contract with Adidas had come to an end. Although Adidas had the right to match what Nike offered, they decided not to, and within days I was decked out in enough Nike stuff for a small army.

I was once again named in the starting line-up for the following two matches against Coventry City at home and then Reading FC away at the Madejski Stadium. We beat Coventry 3-2 in a tough and hard-fought match and then ended up drawing Reading 1-1. The Reading game was also a battle throughout, and the two goals came in rapid succession in the 92nd and 93rd minutes respectively. Darren Bent put us 1-0 up in injury time, and just about everyone in the stadium would have bet on us leaving the stadium with three points. However, Reading had other ideas, and after four passes and a cross from the right, Ivar Ingimarsson managed to secure the equaliser from the kick-off.

The Reading game was a memorable game for several reasons. Two of my friends were travelling around England at the time and managed to get over to watch the game. I rarely got the chance to play in front of friends and family, and it was really special to get to play in front of both Nick and Will and the 23,000 other fans who showed up that day. Nick and I had grown up playing soccer with one another, and it felt great knowing that he was supporting me somewhere within the stadium, although I never knew exactly where he was! Reading's team also included two American players, Bobby Convey and Marcus Hahnemann. Although Bobby was on the bench and didn't make an appearance, the fact that three Americans were involved in such a high level English game spoke volumes for the increasing ability of American players.

Despite drawing with Reading and gaining a point away from home, it really felt as if we had lost. The thought of dropping two points that had seemed ours a minute from the end of the game was sickening. Luckily, our early exit in the FA Cup to Bolton meant we had a two-week break to look forward to before our next game, and the team arranged a trip to Tenerife for a midseason training camp and vacation.

With the season so long and so many games played in such a short period of time during the winter, it was really nice to get a couple of days in the sun. Not many Americans have heard of the island of Tenerife, which is a Spanish island in the Canary Islands off the coast of Morocco, and, to be completely honest, I had no idea where we were going. Only the proper first team players travelled to Tenerife, which meant some of the younger guys who may have trained with the first team sporadically were left behind. Upon our arrival in Tenerife one of the players phoned Scott Mitchell, the youngster who had kept one of the Bolton players onside for one of their goals in our defeat in the FA Cup and who had stayed behind in England. When Mitch answered the phone, the entire team started singing, "One Scotty Mitchell! There's only one Scotty Mitchell! One Scotty Mitchell, there's only one Scotty Mitchell," basically thanking him for our early exit from the tournament that enabled us to have the midseason break. Of course, we meant no malice, but the banter that I had become accustomed to in England makes me laugh to this day.

Despite my geographical naivety, the black sand beaches, fantastic hotel, and amazing weather were all unbelievably recharging. It wasn't all fun and games the whole time, though, and the team met up every day per the manager's instructions for a brisk run and some ball work.

The week we spent in Tenerife was especially good for me because I no longer felt like an outsider around my teammates. I had formed some good friendships with Ian Westlake, Dean Bowditch, and Matt Richards, and the rest of my loan period was much easier for me from a social perspective. Unfortunately, the football side of the deal, the most important part, became a bit tougher for me when we returned from Tenerife. Joe Royle had been trying to sign Portsmouth left-back David Unsworth on loan for a while to strengthen the squad, and the deal had finally been completed upon our return to England. Unsworth, an experienced player who had spent his entire career playing in the Premiership with Everton, West Ham, and Portsmouth, brought with him a fantastic attitude and a wealth of knowledge that only fourteen years in the world's toughest league could produce.

The arrival of Unsworth at Ipswich was great news for the fans and the club in general because the final stretch of the season had arrived, and the addition of an experienced Premiership defender could only make things better. I wasn't ready to give up easily, however, and actually signed a two-month extension to my current one-month loan deal in order to do what I could for the club through March 2005. David obviously started the next match against Sheffield United at Bramall Lane, and I found myself back on the bench where I had initially started my loan deal. We were back to our winning ways with a 2-0 victory in which our new signing scored on his debut. And so started the mixed feelings that every footballer feels when the team is doing well and the player is seemingly struggling. I was happy that we had secured another three points away from home against one of the toughest teams in the League, but the fact that my 'replacement' had recorded a shutout and even scored while doing so was hardly comforting.

I came on as a sub in our next game against Leicester City at home, unaware that it would be the final minutes I played for the club. Keith Gillespie, Leicester City's right midfielder, and I exchanged some words throughout the final minutes of the game, and I found it funny that he was talking so much trash to a guy who had just come on the pitch. After the game, I put my hand out to say good game to him and he basically punched it out of the way. I laughed and muttered something like, "scoreboard", under my breath because we had just won. I didn't think much of it, but Bam Bam witnessed the whole thing, and within moments my entire team was behind me. The mini bust-up continued into the tunnel, and the following day one of the newspapers reported, "Town Badboy Karbassiyoon Has Bust-Up in Tunnel." At least I went out in fashion!

Unfortunately for the club our win against Leicester on February 12th was the last game we'd get three points from in the month of February. We drew away to Preston 1-1 following the Leicester game and then faced back-to-back losses at home against Watford and Queens Park Rangers. With February out of the way, we travelled to Wigan on March 5th desperately searching for three points in a vital top of the table clash. Wigan and Sunderland were now tied with 69 points and our poor month of February had left us three points behind with 66. A win meant we'd be at least even with Wigan and back in the race for automatic promotion. Ninety minutes and one Wigan goal later, the prospect of automatic promotion seemed to be growing more distant.

The battle for promotion and the fight to avoid relegation is really something special in England and in most other leagues in the world. In England, the top two teams at the end of the each season are automatically promoted to the next league up, while the bottom three teams are automatically relegated to the next league down. The third team to get promoted is chosen via a playoff system that sees the number three team play the number six team, while the numbers four and five teams face off. In the first round of the "playoffs" as they are called, two games are played, so each team gets home field advantage at least once. The team with the most goals over the two games advances to the playoff final. The playoff final is one of the most exciting fixtures of the season regardless of which team you support. The fans all know that their club is ninety minutes away from the promised land of a higher league and the losing team faces another year in the same league they were already in.

Promotion generally means higher wages, higher bonuses, better players coming into the club, and more television time. If a team is unable to stay within the top two all season, the goal is to stay within reach of the playoffs (sixth place and up) because anything is possible once the playoffs start. Historically speaking, teams that finish third in the league struggle to gain promotion because they are so disheartened that they didn't gain automatic promotion. Teams that finish sixth are so excited to be in the playoffs and usually come out with much more energy against their higher-seeded opposition. This promotion and relegation culture makes the last day of the season emotionally stressful for clubs at both ends of the table. Some years the clubs are separated by one or two points at the bottom of the table, and a win on the final match day means survival. Other times, a team that has spent the entire season in the top six may falter in the last game of the season and fall to seventh and out of playoff contention. It's very common to see tears shed from both sadness and happiness as the final minutes unfold.

With all this in mind, it's easy to see why morale at Ipswich was very low after our loss at Wigan. The following day those players who didn't play with the first team or hadn't played with them for a while took part in a reserve team game at the training ground. I was happy to get a game in, but was also faced with a serious decision to make. Even though I was still training with the first team every day and had a spot in the squad that dressed every weekend, if I was going to be playing reserve games it would probably be better to head back to Arsenal and play in the reserves there.

I went to speak with the manager a couple of days after the Wigan game and explained how I felt about the whole situation. Mr Royle was an easy person to speak to and he completely understood that, at the end of the day, I just wanted to play at the highest level I could. He asked me to stay and see out the duration of my loan deal, but I had to take into consideration what was best for me and my career. I had already spoken to my agent and discussed my options, so Arsenal had already been alerted that I would be returning the following day for training.

As I packed my bags and said goodbye to the new friends and teammates I had made, I felt truly lucky to have had the chance to be a part of Ipswich Town Football Club. Many players never get the opportunity to experience what it's like to be in a team that is pushing for promotion, and I'll always fondly remember the highs and lows of the two and half months I spent at Ipswich. Just to give you an idea of how cruel football can be, after spending the majority of the season in first or second place, Ipswich finished the 2004-2005 season in third place and lost to West Ham United, the sixth place team, in the playoffs. Since that season, Ipswich has yet to return to the Premier League.

18. The release

I returned to Arsenal the next day and picked up where I had left off. My left-back spot in the reserves had been occupied by one of the youth team players while I was on loan, but my return meant the inevitable for him, and I found myself back in the home team dressing room at Barnet before I knew it. Back in the reserves I had a newfound confidence in myself because of the first team experience I had gained both with Arsenal and Ipswich. Despite being in the reserves again, the last thing I needed to do was tell myself that I was 'too good for this level'. The moment players start to think they have made it and are too good for any game is the moment their careers will probably turn sour and take a downward plunge. Our March 14th home fixture against Chelsea marked my return, and Jérémie Aliadière scored an incredible hat-trick to lead us to a 3-2 victory over our London neighbours.

Our next match against Portsmouth's reserves was played at the training ground because it had been rescheduled from earlier in the season. The game was special for me because it would be the last game I celebrated scoring a goal in an Arsenal shirt. Gilberto Silva played a through ball to me that I chased down with a defender on my right shoulder. My first touch was a "Cruyff" with my left foot behind my right foot and my second touch was a right-footed finish into the far corner. Several of the first team players had stuck around to watch bits and pieces of our game after their morning session, and Dennis Bergkamp was among the spectators. After the game, he approached me and told me that I had scored a great goal. I must admit, it was nice to hear praise from one of football's biggest legends.

Two days later we hosted Southampton at home, and once again I was named in the starting line-up. Prior to the game I was getting a massage in the physio room at the Underhill, and one of our physios asked me how I was holding up injury-wise. It was the first season I had gone without a big injury and apart from the occasional knock here and there, I was quite happy with the state of my body. I told him I was fine and was happy with the way the season had treated me thus far. Fast forward to the 79th minute and a through ball played to Dexter Blackstock, one of Southampton's incredibly fast and strong strikers. We had just taken a corner and both our centre-backs were completely out of position in the opposing team's box. The ball played to Blackstock cut out the second man we had placed in front of him, and off to the races we went. My starting position allowed me to get my body in a little and slow Blackstock down but he had the ball at his feet and I was the only man apart from our keeper left in the mix. He tried to beat me with his speed and my right-footed tackle stopped the ball dead in its track as Blackstock ran past me. I had the ball at my feet and took a touch forward while looking for my next pass before feeling a mixture of studs and legs come crashing into me from behind.

The tackle itself didn't really hurt because I had become accustomed to the physical nature of English football. The moment I got up, however, I felt a grinding sensation in my knee. I took a couple of steps and continued to feel it. I tried jogging it off and about a minute later realised something bad had happened. I don't think the coaching staff was very pleased to see me coming off, especially because it looked as if I didn't want to play any longer due to the 2-1 score in favour of Southampton, but I knew something was wrong with my knee. Of course, at the time I had no idea just how significant that tackle and the severity of the injury to my joint would be.

I spent the next several days getting treatment at the club and a few more days on the pitches with Tony Colbert and Edu, who was coming back from a cartilage operation himself. Tony is usually in charge of training the players who are coming back from injuries and he tries to create match-like situations with mannequins and boards to emulate movements and impact. I continued to feel my pain and was eventually sent to get an MRI scan at one of the many hospitals in London. Sure enough, the MRI results revealed that I had once again managed to tear my meniscus and would once again require surgery.

So, unfortunately, a reckless tackle in the last ten minutes of a reserve game marked the end of my second season at Arsenal. However, it's all part of the risk any player takes when he crosses the white line, and there was no real point dwelling on the fact that I needed surgery again. I just got on with it, undeterred and still focused on my goals and career. Once the surgery was completed, the battle of rehab lay ahead, and I was more than familiar with what that entailed. On top of that, roughly a month before the end of the season, I was told by the coaching staff that Arsenal wouldn't be renewing my contract for the following season. I had sort of expected it, though, because the several players who had earned another contract in the reserves were already busy negotiating them. But even though I guessed it was coming, it was really tough to hear the words come out and be directed towards me.

Making it at Arsenal was never going to be easy. I arrived in England as a striker and was then converted into a left-back in a move that not only helped the club but also helped me and my development at the next level. The situation was clear, though – Ashley Cole was still quite young and was England's top left-back. Behind him, Gael Clichy, a full year younger than I was, served as his back-up and looked to be the future of Arsenal at that position if anything did happen with Cole. The club obviously cited these reasons, and I accepted them. Of course, it's never easy hearing that you aren't good enough for anything you do in life, but I'd accepted that I'd done everything in my power over the course of two years to make it at one of the world's best clubs.

I continued my rehab at the club until the final day of the Premiership and was scheduled to fly back home the following day. I said goodbye to all the staff who keep Arsenal's training ground operating in spectacular fashion and let the doors close behind me one final time as an Arsenal player. I left with my head held high and not a single thought of failure in my mind.

Though my time at the club could hardly be called easy, I wouldn't have traded being there with any other time in their history. I got the chance to see a team of heroes go 49 games in the best league in the world without a single loss. My first season there, I never actually saw them lose in the League. I'm still proud to have made my three appearances for the club and to have become the first American to score for Arsenal in the process.

I loved my experience at Arsenal. Of course, I would get frustrated at times when I thought I deserved to play or when things weren't going my way, but this was more than offset by the number of positive experiences I gained from my two years in London. Some might say I was unlucky to be at Arsenal at a time when the first team was so good that no one could touch them over the course of three seasons. To be completely honest, though, getting the chance to work with and against such talented players was an honour, and I wouldn't trade it for the world. I knew wherever I would end up next would be completely different from what I was used to, but I was happy that I had been given the chance to be a part of Arsenal during such a special time.

The final night I spent in the city that I had begun to love so much was spent driving around both Enfield and Barnet saying goodbye to all the close teammates and friends I had made the past two years. I made sure I stopped by Noreen's house, the lady who had so kindly taken me in during my trial, to say goodbye to her, her family, and both Philippe and Cesc who were living there at the time. Sebastian Larsson, who had been offered a new contract by the club but was later sold to Birmingham City, and I shared our last supper on his balcony before wishing each other the best of luck and saying goodbye.

The end of the season was usually marked by happiness all round due to the fact that a month-and-a-half break was finally upon us, and a short period of relaxation was imminent. As I sat on my flight from Heathrow to Dulles, however, I couldn't help but feel somewhat anxious and scared about my knee, my future, and everything I'd been fighting for my entire life.

19. Welcome to Lancashire

I spent the majority of my summer at home looking after my knee and found myself constantly on the phone with my agent discussing what the next step was going to be. Because my contract with Arsenal had ended, I was free to speak with any clubs that wanted to sign me. An agent's reputation is mainly created with his work during the transfer window, and Will had several clients he was trying to move in the summer of 2005. I'd speak to him two or three times a week on the phone as well as by email as more and more news came to him. My time in the reserves and first team at Arsenal, as well as my time at Ipswich, had resulted in a lot of exposure for me with various Premiership and Championship teams, and a slew of League 1, League 2, and Conference team representatives were always present at our reserve games, waiting for contracts to run out so they could swoop in and have the players for themselves.

Ideally, I was prepared to go as low as the Championship, but hoped a smaller Premier League side might want me. My time at Ipswich had helped me learn about the other leagues outside the Premier League, and I wanted to stay at a high enough standard to still provide value with the style of play I'd learned over the past two seasons.

One of the major characteristics of a transfer, or a deal that is in the works, is that the deal is never completed until the contract is signed. Speculation surrounds many players all the time, and agents and other representatives of players are generally good at playing the press in order to generate the most publicity for their player. For this reason, it isn't uncommon for a player to be linked with one club in the press and then suddenly sign for a completely different team. A lot of things go on behind the scenes between the clubs, the agent, and the player during discussions and negotiations. Sometimes, however, players don't have agents, and when a club approaches a player to sign him, the club who is signing the player may just ask an agent they frequently work with to carry out the deal. In this case, the agent may or may not remain the player's agent once the deal is finalised, but generally is well rewarded regardless for completing the deal.

With that said, Will would call with news that clubs like Derby County, Leicester City, Bournemouth, and others were expressing interest in me. The list of teams would change depending on whether or not those teams had signed someone in my position or were just no longer interested. Some teams wouldn't want to meet my wage demands, while others requested I come on trial before any decisions were made. It was a very interesting time because offers from different parts of the country were being lobbed my way, but I was kind of disappointed that no Championship teams from London had expressed an interest. I knew deep down that the likelihood of me getting to stay in London was small, but I still hoped that one of the clubs in the capital would be after my signature.

I flew back to London several weeks before pre-season started because Will had arranged meetings with several Championship teams. I also rang the Arsenal physios to ask if they would look at my knee once I got back into London to make sure my rehab was progressing steadily. Several days after arriving back in London, Will and I were on our way to Bournemouth, a town on England's southern coast, to meet up with Steve Cotterill, the manager of Burnley Football Club at the time, as well as Tony Pulis, the manager of Stoke City Football Club.

Our first stop was a hotel in Bournemouth where we were scheduled to meet up with Steve Cotterill. Burnley's manager explained that the team was undergoing a massive change and that there were only nine contracted first teamers at the time. He obviously had a lot of players whom he planned on signing and a lot of other players he had in mind, but the opportunity to play would be very good because the previous year's left-back, Mo Camara, had just signed with Celtic Football Club in Scotland. I had no idea where Burnley was on a map but was excited about the idea of first team football and, therefore, agreed to drive up to Lancashire to check out the stadium and training ground in a week's time.

After meeting up with Steve Cotterill, Will and I met with Tony Pulis to discuss a possible deal with Stoke City. Unfortunately the meeting with Mr Pulis was very short because he was in a somewhat tricky situation. His future as manager of Stoke was in question, and he basically told me that he would love to sign me but wasn't sure whether or not he was going to be fired within the next couple of days. Sure enough, a couple of hours after our meeting, Sky Sports News reported that he had been sacked and would not be managing Stoke in the upcoming season. The cut-throat nature of the industry certainly hit home. For players and managers alike, if someone wasn't doing their job well enough, clubs would move quickly to find the best possible replacement and go from there. Between injury and bad results, it was clear to see that everyone was replaceable.

Will advised me that Burnley probably wouldn't let me leave the club without my signature on a contract, so we knew we had a lot of work to do in the upcoming week to make sure that the Burnley option was the best. At that point, Burnley's offer had been the most serious, and although I didn't know much about the club or its location in England, I knew it was a great chance for me to play in a good Championship level team. The only other team that was still in the running was Ipswich Town, and I felt excited the moment Will told me that I had a chance to re-join the Tractor Boys. I had really enjoyed my time at Ipswich and was hoping they would possibly be interested in signing me permanently now that I was out of contract. After Will spoke to Joe Royle,

122

he explained to me that Ipswich was in fact interested and would be able to confirm everything after a meeting to be held on Friday of the following week.

The fact that Ipswich was interested was great news for me, but it also presented a bit of a problem. I was expected to be in Burnley on Wednesday, and Steve Cotterill said that if I didn't sign by Wednesday, then the deal would be off. This really forced me to think things over, because Ipswich hadn't guaranteed anything and Burnley had already put an offer down on the table. I knew what to expect at Ipswich: a fantastic club, a town in which I was comfortable, and teammates I knew and got along with. Unfortunately I didn't know for sure if I would actually be getting all that because they hadn't officially offered me a contract. The only thing I knew about Burnley was that, according to Google Maps, it was somewhere near Manchester and about three and half hours away from London. That is by no means a negative statement about Burnley - it's just that my geography of the United Kingdom was terrible and the only two places I seemed to really know were London and Ipswich.

I had a tough decision to make, and after sitting on it for a couple of days I decided I was going to take Burnley up on their offer. Dave Kevan, the club's assistant coach, called me on Tuesday night and gave me all the details for the next day's visit. The following day I packed my bags, hopped into my car, and started my three-and-a-half-hour journey towards the north west of England. I hadn't really seen all that much of England apart from various stadiums and airports, so the drive was actually quite interesting. After leaving the busy streets that make up the massive metropolis that is London, I soon found myself driving along rolling hills in England's countryside. I knew Burnley was near Manchester, but as I got closer I saw signs for Bolton, Blackburn, and Manchester all within very close proximity to one another. I couldn't believe that there were so many big teams in such a confined area of the country. On top of that, the cities of Preston and Liverpool were also nearby, with Leeds too only a short drive away.

The town of Burnley, which is made up of roughly 75,000 people and lies within the county of Lancashire, is located in a valley surrounded by large rolling hills known as moors. It was definitely very different from what I was used to seeing in London, but it was a welcome change and probably more similar to what I was used to back in Roanoke. Dave told me to meet him at the Dunkenhalgh Hotel in Accrington, one of the most comfortable hotels I've ever stayed in, so that he could take me to the stadium and show me around. Burnley would pay for up to three months of my hotel expenses, and then it was up to me to find an apartment or house to move into. Little did I know that first day, that by the end of my three month stay at the "Dunk", I'd be borderline stir-crazy and ready to get out of the hotel at any cost!

After meeting up with Dave and making the short ten-minute drive up to Burnley, I found myself standing in the reception and back offices of Turf Moor, Burnley's humble and historic 23,000 seat stadium. When I say the stadium was historic, by no means am I exaggerating. The actual club was founded in 1882, and Turf Moor was first used in 1883, although it has gone through several face-lifts since then. The club has a rich history and can boast that it was one of the twelve clubs that founded the original Football League in 1888.

Dave showed me around the stadium, taking me to the pitch, the locker rooms, the boot room, and various other rooms that were frequently used. We then headed to the physio's room where Andy Mitchell and Claire Judd, the team's physios, conducted my medical.

They ran a series of tests on my lungs, heart, and joints, and then took various measurements to see what injuries I would be susceptible to given the natural makeup of my body. The whole process took roughly an hour, and after getting the green light from the physios and having a brief chat by the pitch with Dave, we went upstairs to meet the manager where I signed my two year contract, officially becoming a Claret in the process. I had to sign several other things as well, and I laughed when the club secretary said, "This is to confirm that if we do get relegated, then you'll suffer a decrease in wages. But just to let you know, we won't get relegated at Burnley. So don't even think about it." I laughed because not only was her accent different from anything I'd ever heard, but her attitude went from joking and sincere while I was signing everything else, to extremely serious when the topic of relegation was brought up. It was nice to see the people at the club took their football so seriously, and it was very apparent how much the club meant to them.

Shortly after signing my contract, I headed back down to the pitch and gave my first interview with the club's website. I was also handed a number three shirt with my name on the back and posed for pictures alongside the pitch. As soon as the club had made the announcement that they had signed me, the news was splashed all over the local and national newspapers, as well as being displayed on Sky Sports as one of Burnley's latest signings. I was really excited to have finally completed everything and even overlooked the fact that, despite being the middle of the summer, the temperature was roughly fifty degrees as rain steadily fell to the ground from a grey sky that didn't quite seem to understand that it was meant to be blue in June.

The club continued to sign players as the summer went on, and, before we knew it, a squad of roughly eighteen players had been put together. John Spicer, one of my former teammates at Arsenal, was also bought from Bournemouth, which made my time at training and my downtime at the hotel much easier. I became good friends with all the new signings, simply because we all found ourselves at the Dunk every day after training with little to do. Along with Spice, Burnley signed two other players from Bournemouth: Garreth O'Connor, a fiery Irishman, and Wade Elliott, a calm Englishman from Southampton. Duane Courtney, our late Telford signing, rounded off the five-man hotel crew. None of us knew the area around Burnley or Accrington at all, and so we found ourselves making dinner dates at the hotel restaurant on a nightly basis. Even though we didn't cause any trouble, it was funny seeing us five sitting at the dinner table every night, while distinguished, nicely-dressed hotel guests seemed somewhat disapproving of our presence.

Although I had signed for the club and was up in Burnley, the start of pre-season was still several days away, and I took the time to explore my surroundings a little. I went into the club every day for treatment and light work-outs for my knee to make sure that it was up to the gruelling weeks that lay ahead. One of the biggest differences that I noted immediately upon arrival at Burnley was the difference in facilities between my new club and former club. The training ground at Arsenal was one of the most state-of-the-art sporting facilities I had ever been to. Everything that players needed was located within the doors of the training ground, and the pitches were incredible. After speaking to the staff at Burnley, I found out that due to the old age and current state of the locker rooms at the training ground, the first team was expected to meet up at the stadium in the mornings, change into their training gear there, and then carpool over to the training facility around 10.10 for a 10.30 start. After training ended around 12.30 or one o'clock, the team would carpool back to the stadium to shower and eat before heading home.

The training ground was quite different from Arsenal's, but Steve Cotterill told me that the club had spent nearly one million pounds on a new a pitch specifically for the first team. The pitch had just been laid and was still settling at the start of pre-season, so we spent all of our time on the three grass pitches that the team had used in previous seasons. In all honesty, the grass was actually in very nice condition at the beginning of pre-season. Unfortunately, however, as pre-season got underway and the rain began falling, the pitches started to get cut up and became very messy. I wasn't terribly bothered about it all, though, because I knew from my time at Arsenal that playing on such manicured pitches was a luxury. I was used to playing on less than perfect pitches as a kid growing up and so didn't really let it get to me.

The first day of pre-season was once again upon me, but with a new season came a new team and a completely different set of players in the dressing room. I had become pretty good friends with both Wade and Garreth because of our time at the hotel (Spice and Duane hadn't signed yet), so it was nice to have at least two players I knew in the dressing room on the first day. That first day of training, I couldn't help but notice how the British and Irish dominated the dressing room. Brian Jensen, our massive Danish goalkeeper aptly nicknamed "Beasty", was the only other player in the squad who wasn't English, Irish, or Welsh. We did have several players who played for Jamaica, as well as Ade Akinbiyi who earned an international cap with Nigeria, but they were all born in England, spoke with English accents, and were effectively British in my eyes.

Another change I soon got used to while being at Burnley was the age difference in the team. Reserve team players are usually anywhere from sixteen to twenty one, but there are no age limitations on a first team squad. It was very different coming into training every day and having teammates who were married and had entire families to take care of. Many of the players on our team were in their thirties or late twenties, which made the social dynamic of the dressing room a bit different from what I was accustomed to.

Regardless of age and heritage, however, pre-season was the same for everyone, and that meant a lot of running was upon us. I wasn't nearly as fit as I had been the year before because of my end-of-season injury. I couldn't run or work out during the off season and jumping right into fitness training with the rest of the team wasn't the easiest thing I'd ever done. Double sessions were the norm for several weeks on end, and we didn't see balls for almost two weeks. It was quite disheartening walking out onto the pitches and seeing cones, hurdles, dumbbells, and other inanimate objects that couldn't be kicked or rolled like a ball. The work had to be done, though, because the Championship was and still is an incredibly demanding league physically. Many of the teams are considered quite equal talent-wise, and the only edge a team may have is by being physically faster and stronger than their opposition.

Our schedule was very similar to my schedule at Arsenal. Every morning I'd wake up around 8.45 am, have breakfast in the hotel with the other new signings and then make my way to the stadium in the carpool by 9.45. Once at the stadium, I'd walk through a small back door, which led to a long dark corridor that ran the length of the David Fishwick Stand. My first stop would be the kit room on my right where Daz, the kit man, would supply me with my first session's kit and towel. After grabbing my gear, I'd continue down the hallway and make my next stop at the boot room on my left and pick up my boots. The boot room was the last room on the left before the player's tunnel that led to the pitch. After grabbing my boots, I'd make my way into the home team dressing room, which was a square room with roughly sixteen seats and pegs for your clothing. The treatment room was connected to the dressing room. On the opposite side of the tunnel was the away team's dressing room as well as the player's lounge, which is where all the players would go after a match to meet up with their families and friends.

Our morning sessions during pre-season generally lasted an hour and a half or two hours. Once we were done, we'd carpool back to the stadium, shower, get our new training kit from Daz, and head over to the Bob Lord Stand where lunch was provided. After lunch we'd sit around for an hour or so before heading back to the pitches around two or two thirty. If we didn't go to the pitches, we'd go to the gym, which was a public gym stationed right next to the stadium. We'd finish up around four o'clock and head back to the stadium to shower and change before making our way back to the hotel.

At the hotel, I would spend the majority of my time talking to my friends and family from back home on the internet. My body was so worn out from all the running and weightlifting that all I could really manage to do was lift my fingers to type when I made it back to the hotel room. At that time, my brother, a computer engineer and avid web developer, bought me some web space so I could mess around with a blog to keep in touch with everyone from back home. He bought the "dannyk.us" domain name, and I was blogging within a week. I only ever received about fifty to one hundred unique visitors on any given day, but I was happy that my friends were reading about my life and I was able to stay connected with them. That all changed, however, when I unknowingly published a post that honestly could have sparked World War Three.

On a quiet weekday about a month or so into pre-season, I returned to the hotel from training and decided to update my blog. My objective was to give my friends a bit of an idea of whereabouts I was in the world at that point, because most of them knew I was no longer in London. I posted a map of England pointing out Burnley and Accrington specifically. The words that accompanied the map were along the lines of, "It's a bit boring here, but there are road signs everywhere saying Blackburn, Leeds, Manchester, Bolton, Liverpool, and Preston are nearby." I posted my thoughts, closed my laptop and called it a day.

The next day I returned to my blog to see if anyone had commented on the post, and, to my disbelief, saw that I had over nine hundred comments. I didn't really know what was going on so I started reading some of them and soon realised that I may have said the wrong thing. Completely unbeknownst to me (and I'm being serious, I had absolutely no idea), Blackburn and Burnley are two of Lancashire's biggest rivals. Their fans absolutely despise one another, and the fact that one of Burnley's players had stated that he was bored in Burnley but at least Blackburn was nearby, was quite possibly one of the biggest sins ever committed. The thing is, I never really meant to imply that Burnley was boring. I had been cooped up in a hotel for a month in Accrington, a very small town in England, and was just bored with having to put up with myself for extended periods of time every day. The people of Lancashire had spoken, however, but I don't really think they understood how uneducated I was in terms of Lancashire rivalries.

The responses to my post varied greatly and included the thoughts of both Burnley and Blackburn fans. A lot of the Burnley fans probably understood how naive I was in terms of the rivalry and went ahead and explained to me that I should probably hide for quite some time. Other Burnley supporters, enraged by my obvious disapproval of their town and team, seemed to give me every reason to hide. Blackburn supporters chipped in, calling me all sorts of wonderful words I never knew even existed. Boy, I'd really done it. The following day was press day, and the little problem I had on my hands went from being a small isolated flame, to an all-out blaze that threatened to continue burning and terrorising me unless something was done.

All sorts of journalists and photographers were at the stadium to take pictures of the new signings and to get interviews on press day. The media signs up for interview time, and the players basically get called out to conduct their interviews. I gave several interviews expressing how excited I was to be at Burnley and how determined I was to secure my spot in the first team. I fielded questions about the changes I was facing coming from such a large Premiership team to a middle of the table Championship side. Everything seemed normal until the reporters started asking me about my blog and why I had made such a bold statement to the world.

So that was good. My innocent, "I'm kind of bored and lonely", post had attracted several thousand visitors to my site who felt inclined to tell me I was an idiot in over a thousand comments. I guess the only positive was that I had put *dannyk.us* on the map and, through one post, had increased my site traffic by about 5000%. The site ended up crashing for a little when my allotted bandwidth was exceeded, which gave me a little bit of time to think about my next move. I posted an apology and an explanation on my site a day later and was asked by Steve Cotterill to take the site down shortly thereafter.

Despite the abrupt end to my makeshift blogging career, the soccer continued and we were well into the middle of pre-season. Our first pre-season friendly was against Cheltenham Town FC, where I started on the bench and was given the last twenty minutes on the pitch. The game went fine for me and I enjoyed making my first appearance for my new club, but it was the first game I had played in since my last knee surgery and I was very susceptible to other injuries. My knee felt fine throughout the game, but during the final minutes I felt a very strange and painful feeling in my hip.

I didn't really think anything of it, but I felt it again the next day in training, and it felt almost as if something inside my hip had become detached. We travelled ten minutes down the road four days later to play Accrington Stanley, a local Conference team, which attracted many fans from both Accrington and Burnley. I was still struggling with my injury, and while I sat on the team bench numerous fans kept approaching me and asking me what had happened to my blog. At least the people wanted more! Several days later we hosted Spanish La Liga side Malaga in our first match at Turf Moor before packing our bags on the team coach, driving to Liverpool airport, and flying to Austria for our pre-season camp.

We flew into Salzburg, an Austrian city that lies just next to Germany on the border, and then took a bus to Obertraun, an incredibly scenic and wonderfully clean town in the middle of some of the highest mountains I've ever seen. Our final destination was a sports-specific training centre complete with bedrooms, a gym, multiple pitches, and a restaurant. The isolated locale allowed the team to focus on our work for the week and on the season ahead. We began training the day we arrived, and due to the fact that my pain still hadn't eased, I joined the physios and several other injured players who were getting back to fitness. Once again I was incredibly frustrated with my body, which forever seemed to be letting me down. I had played a total of twenty minutes so far in pre-season friendlies, and I was missing a massive opportunity to solidify my spot in the starting eleven. One of the toughest parts was trying to convince the staff and my teammates, a group of guys whom I had known for only a couple of weeks, that I really was injured and wasn't trying to get out of all the hard work that made up pre-season.

I spent the rest of the week getting treatment and sitting on the side-lines as my new team played in two more friendlies before making the forty-five minute drive back to Salzburg and flying back to Liverpool. The week had been hard for everyone, including me. Despite being injured, I spent a lot of time with the physios strengthening my upper body and running. I found myself able to run the whole week, but as soon as I went to kick a ball, the sharpest of pains would shoot through my hip as I winced in pain. After returning to Burnley I was scheduled to see several specialists throughout Lancashire and continued treatment at the club. The season had started on August 6th, and we were handed our first two losses of the season, first by Crewe Alexandra in Crewe and then at home to Sheffield United. Andy Mitchell and I spent a lot of time in his BMW driving up and down north east England's extensive motorway system visiting hip and groin specialists. I saw three specialists and received three injections into my hip before seeing one specialist who was able to locate the source of my pain as soon as I told him the discomfort I was feeling. One stinging injection into a very unpleasant region of my midsection later and I was relieved of pain and able to take part in training within a couple of days.

Unfortunately for me and my chances of securing Burnley's starting left-back spot, it was already October and the season was well underway. It had been so frustrating coming to the stadium every match day and travelling with the team to away games only to sit in the crowd and cheer my teammates on. The left-back spot was still up for grabs, and the fact that my injury took so long to mend devastated me mentally. Several weeks before getting back into training, Jon Harley, a former Chelsea, Fulham, West Ham, and Sheffield United left-back, signed for us and basically confirmed the fact that I wasn't going to be guaranteed anything in the team when I reached fitness again. Jon brought with him a wealth of experience from both the Premiership and Championship and effortlessly slid in to the left side of our defence. It was tough for me to see that we had obviously signed a player who was playing in my position, but I had nothing against Jon and the competition we had between us was only ever healthy.

Prior to Jon Harley signing for Burnley, I really believed that I was going to be able to get regular time in the first team once I was fit again and could train regularly with the team. I wasn't, but I was determined enough and believed in myself enough to think that I was worthy of being in the starting eleven. A week after the injection, the team travelled to Selhurst Park in London to face Crystal Palace. I was named to the bench, which was a good starting point for my return, but failed to get into the game that ended in a 2-0 loss for us.

Three days later, we were scheduled to travel to Birmingham to play Aston Villa at Villa Park. The entire first team squad was required to travel on match days, regardless of fitness. For away matches that were several hours away, we'd travel the night before and stay in a hotel. If our opponents were located near us, we'd travel directly to the stadium from Turf Moor on the day of the match. Cotterill would usually announce the starting eleven and those players on the bench during our pre-match meeting at the hotel. Those players left out of the squad would still have to warm up with the team and then shower and sit in the crowd once warm-ups were over and the match was about to begin.

I knew I wouldn't be starting against Villa because I wasn't completely match-fit yet and was happy to be named to the bench. I had played sixty minutes in one reserve team match prior to our encounter with Crystal Palace, but I was ready to give everything I had if I was called into the match from the bench. I always enjoyed both the Carling Cup and FA Cup matches we played in because our opponents usually weren't Championship teams. I had been to Villa Park the year before to see Arsenal play Manchester United in an FA Cup Semi-Final, so I knew what Villa Park was all about and was very excited to get the chance to play there. Just under 27,000 fans came out to Villa Park on October 25, 2005, about 4,000 of them Burnley fans. Villa put out a strong team including names like Juan Pablo Ángel, Gareth Barry, James Milner, and Olof Mellberg. Kevin Phillips put the Villains ahead after twenty-two minutes and we spent the majority of the match fighting for an equaliser without creating many chances. I began warming up in the latter part of the second half, hoping that I'd get the chance I desperately wanted. With fifteen minutes to go, the coaching staff had me replace Wade Elliott and I slotted into the left midfield spot.

I was happy and relieved to finally make my official Burnley debut, and I was hoping that the coincidence of making my Arsenal debut and scoring on it almost exactly a year before would bring me some sort of luck. It was a great feeling being under the lights in front of so many people again, and I really wanted to change the game in a positive manner for us. My performance wasn't only important for me, but I wanted to repay the supporters and the staff for having been so patient with me during my injury-laden time. I did my best to keep the ball whenever I had it but had to do a lot of work defensively, making sure that James Milner wasn't allowed free rein down their right-hand side.

With several minutes left to play, a ball was played into Villa's box from our right-hand side. The box was full of bodies from both teams, and a clear path to the goal was almost nowhere to be found. Gifton Noel-Williams, one of our big, strong strikers, tried to meet the cross in the air but was knocked slightly off balance by one of Villa's defenders. As a result, the ball was knocked down to me at the edge of the box. Two Villa players rushed towards me, and I didn't think twice as I hit a left-footed volley that took a slight deflection and nicked the crossbar before going out for a corner. Unfortunately that shot could've summed up my luck at Burnley up to that point. In training I was very comfortable hitting shots like the one that had just been presented to me, and I was confident when I hit it that I'd be celebrating a goal and completely changing the course of the match. Instead, we ended up heading to the locker room and having to deal with a 1-0 loss and an early exit from the Carling Cup. Mark Yates, the reserve team manager and one of the first team's assistant coaches, was happy and positive about my performance, and his kind words helped salvage the little bit of confidence I still had in myself.

Training continued and my knee and hip both started feeling much better. I was training hard and was really enjoying my time at the training ground. Although I had only featured in one first team match, I had dressed and made the bench for every game since I had returned from injury. After the Villa match, the team went on a four-game winning streak against Hull City, Millwall, Luton Town, and Leicester City, and I knew I'd have to wait for us to slip up a little before I got my chance. At the time, the manager had basically made up his mind about nine or ten players he wanted in his starting line-up, and he only ever really rotated one of the outside midfielders depending on their performances in training and the previous match. Because we were winning, he had very little to think about selection-wise and continued using the same eleven players from match to match.

It would take almost a month before I would get another taste of first team football, and Elland Road, Leeds United's 40,000 seat stadium, provided the stage for the rough and tough fixture. I looked forward to the Leeds match in particular because I had watched Leeds play there in the Champions League on television several years before and knew just how much history the ground had. It was crazy to think that Leeds, a team that would have made the Champions League Final in 2001 if they had beaten Valencia in the semi-finals, had fallen victim to England's unforgiving relegation system and faced the drop to the Championship in the 2003-2004 season. What's even more shocking is the fact that they weren't able to bounce back up to the Premiership straight away, suffered a widely publicised financial crisis shortly after, were relegated again several years later, and spent a couple of seasons in League 1 before finally getting promoted to the Championship again where they find themselves as of 2015.

I had been training well at that point of the season and was itching to get on the pitch, especially after David Healy and Robbie Blake had both scored two second-half goals to put Leeds ahead. In the 78th minute I replaced Spice and made my way to left side of the midfield. We were doing everything we could to get back into the game and, with little time left, a 1 v 1 opportunity presented itself to me on the left side of Leeds' box that I gladly accepted. I ran at Gary Kelly, Leeds' veteran right-back, with confidence and pace and edged past him before cutting back inside to create an angle for myself to shoot. The opportunity to shoot had passed, however, and I passed the ball into a crowded heap of players in the middle of that box that ended in a defensive clearance. My decision-making had been poor, and I was surprised at myself for having passed in that situation instead of shooting. The game ended several minutes later, and back in the dressing room the manager came over to me and asked me why I didn't shoot. I responded, "I don't know", and I could tell that my response was not what he was looking for at all. Then again, I don't think I could have said anything that would have pleased him at that point, and he went on to yell at me about how I would have taken that shot in training and that's what training was for. I didn't really have anything to say, so I just nodded until he was done with me and moved on.

I was pretty upset to know that, despite being on the pitch for only twelve minutes, the manager had decided to pick on me first in the dressing room. Sure, I should have shot when I had the chance - a ninetieth-minute goal for us could have provided a lifeline, but I was on the pitch for twelve minutes, while ten other players had just spent ninety minutes on the pitch without scoring. I didn't mind being yelled at, I was used to that whole aspect of the game by that point, but I would have liked to think that the manager would have possibly seen the fact that after only being on for twelve minutes I had created a scoring opportunity, which was at least something positive that could be taken from my performance. Nope, the fact that I'd blown it was far more important, and so I boarded the bus wondering how long I'd have to wait before I got my next opportunity to impress the coaching staff.

I didn't have to wait as long as I had imagined, however, and was brought on as sub in the 89th minute in our three nil victory over Crewe at home four days later. Even though I was coming on as a sub, I was ecstatic to be a part of the team. Win or lose, it was always mentally reassuring for me to know that I had taken part and done my best in the game. Sitting on a bench for ninety minutes was hardly fulfilling and became repetitive very quickly. Mentally, it was hard not to get the wrong attitude even though I began to realise that I wasn't probably going to get any more than ten minutes of playing time, if that, on any given match night.

As the season continued, the players who weren't playing regularly in the first team were asked to play in the reserves on Wednesday nights. Once again, it was very tough mentally to suit up with players whose average age was around seventeen and play in tiny stadiums with awful pitches that no one seemed to care about. I tried my best to put those thoughts aside, however, and gave every match as much as I could. I admit now that my performances in the reserves at Burnley weren't the best. I was so used to playing wonderful, flowing football at Arsenal, and the pitch conditions and style of play that were being presented to me here were not really what I was used to. Every match was a grind, a battle that would usually end with more knocks than a first team game, but I persevered. The saving grace for me was that by that point in the season, several of the hotel crew had also been left out of the starting eleven for quite some time, and we'd all have to play in the reserves together.

In one reserve game in particular, the reserves were missing several youth team players and I was asked to play centre-back alongside Duane Courtney. I agreed because by that point I was just happy to get a game, but I remember looking at Duane and thinking, "this could be catastrophic." I'd never played centre-back in my life, had only learned how to play a defensive position in general the year before, and had to deal with a striker who reminded me of an NFL line-backer. To be completely honest, I thought I did okay all things considered. The pitch at Accrington Stanley was a joke by that point of the season (almost the entire penalty area had sand thrown down on it to help ease the mud situation), and we ended up conceding a couple of goals because the ball would completely die on the pitch, ruin our positioning, and eventually punish us.

After the game ended, as I sat in the cold, damp, dressing room with my first game as a centre-back under my belt, I saw Mark Yates and Steve Cotterill walk in. As I said, I didn't think I had done all that badly all things considered, and I wasn't really expecting to be singled out on this rare occasion. Mark Yates expressed his disapproval to the team, which was to be expected, before the gaffer started criticising all the first team players who took part in the game.

One by one he went down the line basically telling us how badly we had played. In all fairness, he was right. We hadn't played well at all, but the conditions were woeful, and we were all very well aware of the fact that we had been garbage that night. When he got to me, he spent some time telling me that I had no idea where I was on the pitch throughout the match, and that I had been completely outclassed by a player who wasn't anywhere near good enough to make it at the top level. It was getting increasingly hard to win the manager's approval of my ability, and I began wondering if it would ever actually happen.

The month of November had come and gone, and I was unable to convince anyone at the club to cook me turkey for Thanksgiving. Apparently the English don't celebrate the whole idea of the Pilgrims leaving England and coming to the United States to find a better life. I spent all the games leading up to Christmas on the bench as an unused substitute and, for the first time in my life, wasn't even bothered about the fact that Christmas was upon me. The only thing I was looking forward to was seeing the end of 2007, because several of my friends had planned to come visit me over the post-Christmas and New Year period. I was having a tough time with football and needed more than anything to see my friends from home and get a dose of reality.

Before the hectic Christmas period was finally upon us, the team arranged a visit to one of the local children's hospitals. The club provided us with big Santa hats, and walking through the brightly coloured halls of the hospital really helped me put into perspective just how minute my current problems were relative to the suffering I witnessed in the hospital. Seeing the children's faces light up when players from their favourite team in the world walked into their rooms with presents was something I'll never forget. The parents of the children were in tears as we gave presents to each patient and their siblings. Most of the kids were massive Burnley fans and couldn't express just how happy they were to have the opportunity to meet us, saying it was the best Christmas they had ever had.

My injuries, lack of playing time, and struggle to settle in at Burnley were all pushed aside as we watched children strapped to tubes, IV's, and machines break out into some of the largest smiles I'd ever seen. One little boy in particular made me laugh so hard when he told me in his thick Lancashire accent that he was in no way a Burnley fan, by no means impressed by our arrival at the hospital, and that Blackburn was the best club in the world. Jokingly, I hoped that, for his own sake and well-being, the kid would never become a blogger in the greater Burnley area in the future.

We trained on Christmas Eve as well as Christmas Day, and I was grateful that Wayne Thomas invited me over to his house to have Christmas dinner with his family, because I don't know what I would have done on my own in my flat.

Our December 31st match with Sheffield Wednesday was different from most games because my friends had successfully made it over and would be watching. Also Frankie Simek, my ex-teammate and fellow American from Arsenal, was Sheffield Wednesday's starting right-back. I made a brief ten-minute appearance at the end of our 2-1 defeat, but I was happy that I at least made it onto the pitch for the only game that my friends would ever be able to see me play in. After the game one of my friends asked me why someone in the crowd had called me a "donkey" when I was on the ball, and I tried to persuade him that the word "donkey" was used as a positive name for players in England. It didn't take long for me to realise that my friend wasn't an idiot, and we all laughed at the fact that a fan of my own team had called me a jackass. It was nice having my friends from home around, and my performance in training greatly reflected the fact that for a couple of weeks I was carefree and enjoying my football again.

Once again, I had to wait nearly a month to make my next appearance before coming on as a sub for the last twenty minutes against Preston North End at home. Due to Preston's close proximity to Burnley, the match was highly anticipated and drew a larger crowd than normal. On my way to the stadium, as I passed under an overpass on the highway, I noticed roughly thirty police cars and motorcycles parked on the bridge. Security around Turf Moor was much higher than it was generally, and the atmosphere during the game explained why so many police units had been needed.

I didn't make an impact during my twenty minutes on the pitch and was more frustrated with myself than anyone or anything else. Playing such a small role with the first team was very tough mentally for me. The preparation and mindset as a sub was completely different from that as a player on the pitch, and, although I did my best to prepare myself both physically and psychologically before each match, it was very tough expending so much energy focusing on everything when there was a ninety percent chance that the only action I'd see during the game was from the side-line whenever I was told to warm up.

I started second-guessing my ability and myself just as I had at Arsenal during my first season in England, and my mindset drastically changed. I lost all confidence in myself as a player and actually started wondering if the problem was just the fact that I wasn't good enough. My agent asked the manager if I was free to go out on loan several times, and each time I was told that I couldn't leave.

I wanted to do everything I could for Burnley, but was getting old very quickly just sitting on the bench and losing every ounce of belief I had spent twenty-one years building for myself. I felt as if I had disappointed myself, my family, and everyone else who knew me, including the fans who came out to see the team play every week.

Months earlier during pre-season, as we left Turf Moor on a coach headed to the airport, I saw a fan wearing a shirt with my name and number on it. He waved at me on the bus and turned his back to me, pointing at my name and smiling the whole time until we were out of sight. It was people like these that I felt I was letting down, and I wanted more than anything to change it. Every home game, after parking my car in the designated player's parking lot, it was typical that fans would crowd the stadium entrance and ask for autographs. They would always ask me when I was going to get to play, and I desperately wished I had an answer for them. Thankfully for my own health and mental peace, I was able to hold on to the positives from everything I had accomplished up to that point in England and continued working as hard as I could in training.

Even though it was strange having such an age difference in my teammates, I found speaking to the older and more experienced guys quite comforting. They had been in my shoes before and helped me greatly throughout this turbulent time. Danny Coyne, John McGreal, and Graham Branch in particular seemed to be able to sense what I was going through and were always giving me words of encouragement. I wasn't looking for sympathy by any means, but I needed to hear some sort of positive encouragement in what seemed to be a world filled with plenty of negatives at the time. Danny Coyne urged me to continue working hard and kindly told me that I had the quality to play in the Premiership eventually. He could definitely see that I was very close to giving in to the hardships that can surround professional footballers, and the last thing he wanted me to do was lose all hope in everything I had ever worked for.

As the season powered on towards April, training continued and the coaching staff did a good job of mixing things up to break the monotony and keep our concentration levels where they needed to be. On one particular day an ITV camera crew showed up at our training ground and told us that the team needed to select one player to complete a challenge they had going on with a large number of clubs throughout the country. The challenge consisted of hitting a handful of balls from different locations about twenty-five to thirty yards away from the goal. The first ball was placed on the end line to one side of the goal, and the series of balls arced around the goal with the final ball being placed on the opposite side of the goal to the first ball. The rules stated that the ball had to cross the line before bouncing, and any miss would add three seconds to the final time.

Frank Sinclair, our captain, was given the honour of selecting the player who would take part in the challenge and, after asking the team their opinion, decided that I would be the right contestant for our team. The team's reasoning was that I could use both feet equally well and that I would be able to curl the two end line balls into the goal with relative ease. Frank introduced me to the cameras as Burnley's "All American Superstar", and a microphone was attached to my training kit before I made my way to the first ball. The entire team stood behind the goal, cheering me on, as three cameramen pushed their record buttons and began videotaping. I was told that as soon as I made contact with the first ball the timer would start and couldn't have been more disappointed with myself when I saw my first effort hit the post and rebound wildly off the pitch. I grabbed another ball and accurately placed my next shot where it needed to be before jogging to the next ball. After making my way around the arc, I ended up with only one more missed opportunity and finished pretty quickly. A six-second penalty was added to my score, which ended up being good enough for the third place in the country. The team rejoiced, and I was lifted and carried around like a king for about twenty seconds before being dropped on the pitch. Regardless of my form and situation at the club, I trained with a smile on my face that day and thoroughly enjoyed the banter and camaraderie from all my teammates.

I put my head down and continued on with the season as best as I could. True to the other games that I had played in, my appearance against Preston seemed to mean that I would have to wait four games before playing my next meaningful minutes in a Burnley shirt. An injury to Graham Branch in the 39th minute in our away fixture against Coventry on February 25th meant I'd get my first lengthy spell in a match, and I was incredibly excited when I was told I was going in. I had no time to warm up, as I was sitting on the bench sipping on a Powerade when Branchy went down, so my introduction to the game was brought on quite hastily. It was a wonderful day for football – the sun was actually shining, and the roughly 20,000 supporters who filled Coventry's brand new Ricoh Arena provided a perfect atmosphere for the middle of the table match.

We had only won one game in our last eight matches, and our last victory away from home had come in November when we miraculously beat Luton Town 3-2 after having our goalkeeper sent off and replacing him with a field player. Our form obviously wasn't the best and it showed. Coventry dominated the majority of the game, and we left the Ricoh Arena on the wrong side of a 1-0 score line. Once again, I hadn't really played poorly, but I hadn't done anything outstanding and probably didn't give the manager any reason to change his opinion about me.

With April 30th and the end of the season only two months away, I did my best to keep as positive as I could and was looking forward to my summer break at home. I wasn't really sure what the coaching staff thought about my future, although I did have a general idea from the way my first season at the club had gone. I spent the remainder of the season's matches on the bench, making several appearances in the reserves until the last game of the season was upon me. We drew with Luton Town 1-1 at home and ended up finishing 17th in the table, 12 points above the relegation zone. The season had been a long roller-coaster ride for both the team and me. Although we spent the majority of the season in the middle of the pack, we did dabble with a spot in the playoffs for several weeks, but also faced relegation in the bottom three of the League for a couple of weeks as well.

20. Back to square one

After the match with Luton Town, we reported to training for two more days in order to complete the yo-yo running test to measure our fitness levels. The results from the test would be used as a benchmark for the following season in order to evaluate our overall endurance. Even though I hadn't played in a first team match since February, I was still quite fit and finished second in the team behind Andy Gray. I met with the coaching staff after our final session at Turf Moor in order to discuss my first season and what I should expect for my second and final year of my contract. We all agreed that placing me on the transfer list was the best option for all parties involved, and I was relieved to know I'd be able to put the previous year behind me and begin my search for a new team.

While some people on the outside may look at a player being put on the transfer list as a form of rejection, it is often the best for both parties. Players who are doing well at a club, playing weekly, and at a challenging enough level or club are rarely put on the transfer list, whereas players who are either finding it difficult to settle or break into the team will find themselves on the transfer list. With the career window in the game being so short, it is usually in the best interests of a player to get himself into a situation where both he and the club are happy that he is there.

Though I hate having any regrets, at times I did look back and wish things at Arsenal had worked out differently even at this stage. I was finally feeling comfortable in London when my contract did come to an end, and I just couldn't help but think that my career was meant to go a different way after my first year at my new club.

When a team places a player on the transfer list, other teams are alerted that the player and his current club are willing to part company, and the player can begin his search for a new team. Depending on how high-profile the player and how desperate the club is to get rid of the player, transfer fees may or may not be placed on a player. If a player hasn't really played much at his current club, then the player's stock will drastically drop, and he may be able to leave for much less than he was worth prior to that season. The complete opposite can happen if a player has a breakout season which causes his worth to skyrocket. One of Arsenal's most famous pieces of fiscal work surrounded the signing and selling of Nicolas Anelka. After buying Anelka from Paris Saint Germain in 1997 for £500,000 (roughly $800,000), the club sold him two years later for £22.3 million (roughly $39 million). Making £21.8 million pounds in a two year span from the transfer of a player, or any investment at that, is incredible and can help fund the purchase of other players or other club developments.

Once two teams have decided on a fair price for a player, the club which is purchasing the player will pay the club which currently employs the player the transfer fee. The club that employs the player is responsible for setting the transfer fee, which allows clubs to protect their best players by placing incredibly high transfer fees on them. The player usually receives about 10% of the transfer fee, and the rest is split up between agents, taxes, and other beneficiaries, with the club that is selling the player receiving the biggest chunk of change. The highest transfer in the history of football at the time of writing took place when Real Madrid purchased Gareth Bale from Tottenham in 2013 in a deal worth up to £85 million, or roughly $133 million.

Once a transfer fee has been negotiated and agreed upon, the player and his agent then start negotiating the player's contract. Contracts in England and many other European countries are guaranteed, which makes earning long-term contracts very difficult. If a player signs a three-year contract and gets injured the day he signs, he will still be guaranteed pay for three years as long as the injury wasn't a breach of the terms of the contract.

Once we were given the okay to disperse for our summer break, I made my way back to the States in order to rest and sort out my future. We were given heart rate monitors and a work-out programme to complete over the summer, and I started running and working out per the programme as soon as my two-week rest sequence came to an end. I had parted company with Will, my agent, about six months before and was speaking to several agents who were doing their best to find teams who were interested in me. Because I hadn't played much the previous season, I had virtually received no exposure at Burnley and was finding it difficult to find a club. Transfers are only permitted during the transfer windows, which happen twice a year in the world of football. Although different countries follow different rules, English clubs are allowed to make their transfers from July 1st to August 31st during the summer transfer window, and from January 1st to February 2nd during the winter transfer window. If players who are looking to get out of their current contractual obligations haven't found a club by those dates, they are required to stay with their current teams unless they can sort out a loan deal. I wanted to do everything I could to make sure that I found another club where I was wanted and would hopefully play week in and week out.

Psychologically, I was in quite a strange place. I was returning to a club that I knew, and even hoped, I'd be leaving quite soon, but I was determined and focused on having a good pre-season and just putting the previous year behind me. Pre-season always signified a fresh start, and while I knew I wasn't in the manager's plans for this coming season, I was excited to get back into training and just focus on my future, wherever it might be.

I returned to Burnley on June 24th of 2006, several weeks before pre-season started, in order to receive some treatment on my knee as it had flared up a little since I had been home. I had been running quite a bit in order to get fit for the season ahead, and I apparently did a little too much. Both Wayne Thomas and Danny Coyne were recovering from anterior cruciate ligament injuries, so the three of us spent several weeks together with Claire and Mitch, the team physios, before everyone reported back for the start of pre-season. I wanted to make sure my knee was 100% before starting pre-season, and I wasn't terribly worried about rushing back to impress the staff. Unfortunately, I was expected to take part on the first day with the team and suffered the consequence as my knee swelled back up as soon as our first two sessions had come to an end. My schedule remained the same for the majority of pre-season, I'd train for a day or two, my knee would swell, and I'd rest for three or four days until it settled. Once it settled, I'd train again and then be forced to sit out because of the discomfort. It was incredibly frustrating having to be sporadic with my training, but I was more worried about not being able to train with a team if I was asked to go on trial with a new club.

Several weeks into pre-season, one of the agents I was in contact with let me know that AZ Alkmaar, a team in the Dutch Eredivisie, was interested in me and wanted me to come to Alkmaar for a week's trial. I was excited about the opportunity, but I was hesitant about agreeing to anything because of the state of my knee. I was persuaded to book my flight to Holland after a couple of days and made the short flight to Amsterdam. Training sessions at Alkmaar were exactly what I had expected; the sessions were incredibly technical and I thoroughly enjoyed the change in setting and everything else that accompanied the new club. Just because I was in a new country and at a new club, though, it didn't mean that my knee had miraculously healed, and I started experiencing the same reactions to training that I had back in Burnley.

My trial ended with a game against a team from Amsterdam, and I was told I'd be playing the position of left wing-back, which was different from what I was used to. Although I was expected to defend like a left-back, I was also expected to attack like a left midfielder, and I was more than happy to play a role that allowed me to attack often. The game went well, but my knee didn't enjoy the ninety minutes as much as I had. The following day the agents which had lined up the trial with Alkmaar informed me that, although Alkmaar didn't think I'd be a right fit at their club, several other Dutch club scouts had been at the game and were interested in pursuing my services. I was happy to have impressed someone, but wanted more than anything to figure out what was going on with my knee. I headed back to England contemplating a future in Holland but with the main objective being to get fully fit before doing anything else.

I flew back to England and reported to training with my teammates at Burnley the following day. Most of my teammates were happy that I had been given the opportunity in Holland, stating that my style of play was probably better suited in a more technical country like Holland, rather than the physically demanding Championship in England. Pre-season was in full swing by the time I returned, but that didn't mean the fitness training was over. We continued our tiring running schedule every morning, and played a little bit of football in the afternoons. My knee didn't really hurt, but something was obviously wrong with it, as it was swelling off and on as it had been doing prior to my Alkmaar trial.

Our pre-season tour was scheduled to take place in Bardolino, Italy, and I was excited about the opportunity of travelling to one of Italy's picturesque northern cities. A day or so before the trip to Italy, Aaron McFarling, a journalist from *The Roanoke Times*, my local paper from back home, called and asked if I would give him an interview. Aaron had covered my football career since my high school days, and our conversations were never really like interviews. I spent about thirty minutes talking to him about my previous year, what I was planning on doing next, and how I felt about everything. The following day, the team boarded a plane in Liverpool and we flew to Milan, where we boarded a coach and made our way to Bardolino.

Apart from being injured and requiring treatment the entire time in Italy, I enjoyed the trip for all it was worth. I knew I'd be visiting a specialist and getting an MRI scan as soon as I returned to England, so I did what I could for my knee and spent the majority of the trip in the gym and on the pitches doing weight circuits with Mitch. Halfway through our trip, we were given a day off to visit Verona, relax, or check out what Lake Garda had to offer. After spending the day in Verona with most of the team, we all returned to the hotel in time for curfew. As we walked into the hotel, I noticed the entire staff was seated by one of the coffee tables in the lobby. Steve Cotterill asked me to take a seat with the rest of the staff, and I was kind of confused as to what was going on. Apparently someone had given the manager the interview that I had given in *The Roanoke Times,* and he wasn't very happy with the way the article had come out. Given that *The Times* was my local paper and the purpose of the article was to update the people in the Roanoke Valley about my progress as a professional in England, the article was biased in my favour. I was scolded for the interview and everything that I had said in it. The manager was extremely unhappy with me, and I think the article was probably the piece of straw that broke the camel's back. A lot of the players on the team were playing pool in the room adjacent to the lobby and heard the commotion that was taking place. I listened to what he had to say, made a couple of remarks of my own, and then made my way to my room.

The rest of the trip was miserable. A lot of my teammates had heard what happened and weren't particularly inclined to speak with me in public out of what seemed like fear of the consequences. Of course, when we were in hotel rooms, they all asked what exactly had happened and offered advice as to what I should do.

That week in Italy was one of the strangest weeks of my life. I was 21 years old and felt as if I was 10. I not only respected everyone around me, but I felt as if I'd earned the respect of both my teammates and the staff in the time I'd been at Burnley. To be treated this way felt so strange. I couldn't wait for the trip to end and to return to

England where there was at least some sense of normalcy and my teammates would be able to acknowledge my existence.

Whether or not Steve Cotterill felt the way I did, I can't be sure, but I felt as if the argument solidified the fact that I had to leave Burnley as soon as I returned to England. Mentally I was so tired of everything I had experienced, and the stress I was feeling wasn't doing my physical health any good. The team returned to England after several friendlies and a week's worth of training in Italy. I was scheduled for my knee scan as soon as we were back in Burnley, and I would then see a knee specialist several days later to discuss the results of the scan. Mitch and I hopped in his BMW after training on a rare dry day in August of 2006 and made our way to the doctor the club used to assess knee injuries. I had become so accustomed to hospitals, clinics, injections, scans, and everything else regarding injuries, that I was simply expecting to hear that I had a slight tear in my meniscus and would require a joint clean out in order to be comfortable again. Unfortunately, the news was far more drastic. After reading the MRI report, the doctor simply said, "The report says there is nothing structurally wrong with your knee." I sighed with relief and may even have smiled, thinking that I didn't require surgery and just needed an extended period of rest. The doctor followed his first statement by saying, "Unfortunately, that means your knee is knackered (finished) and you should probably consider hanging up your boots."

Hearing the doctor use the words he did caught me completely off guard, and a feeling of complete helplessness took over me. Once my initial shock ended, the only thing I wanted to do was get out of the doctor's office and get to a place where I could think things through and speak to my family. I could tell that even Mitch was shocked to hear what the doctor had just said with such ease. Mitch and I left the doctor's office shortly after and were back on the highway, making the forty-five minute drive back to Burnley before I knew it. Tears welled in my eyes as I sat in the passenger seat of his car, silent, staring at nothing in particular on the road ahead of me. My initial annoyance at having to find a new club and rebuild my career were dwarfed by the fact that I might never be able to play football again. As we pulled into the town of Burnley, Mitch sighed and said, "Well that was a lot to take in." I told him that I'd fight it and be playing again as soon as I got myself sorted out. I pushed the thought of having to stop playing out of my head and was almost insulted at the idea of quitting. We pulled into the club's parking lot where I climbed into my car and started my drive home.

As soon as I got home, I called my parents and told them I was coming back to the States. I explained what the doctor had told me, and we all agreed that my problem was no longer simply with football. I had to fix my general health, and I wanted to do that in the United States. I was told by the doctor before I left that I should take six to eight weeks of mandatory rest and see if that improved the state of my knee. From there I could possibly get back into a light training regime and see how my body would react to everything. I was adamant about leaving, however, and didn't want to spend another six to eight weeks in the gym at Burnley.

The following day I arranged to meet with Steve Cotterill after training and told him that I would be willing to leave the club for less money than I was guaranteed on my contract. I had signed a two-year deal, and given that my second year had just begun, I was still guaranteed an entire year's worth of pay if I chose to stay the whole year. I had no intention of staying, however, and after about a week of negotiations I was given a lump sum, thus ending my tenure with Burnley Football Club. My final meeting with Cotterill wasn't as hostile as I thought it had the potential to be. We had our own thoughts about my time at the club, and since everyone is entitled to their own opinion, I heard him out. We agreed that I should come in on August 19th for our game against Wolverhampton Wolves as a way to say my final goodbye to all my teammates.

As soon as I left Turf Moor after negotiating my exit, the team website announced that I had parted company with the club. I had barely eaten lunch and made it home before the news was made public, but I was just happy to know that I was heading home to fix my knee and ultimately fix my future. I had been speaking to several Major League Soccer teams at that point and, if all went to plan, I'd be able to join the MLS and start playing as soon my injury nightmares could be put behind me. After parking my car in the player's lot before the match with Wolves, a good number of the fans who were always seeking autographs, handshakes, and pictures at the player's entrance asked me about my departure, why I was leaving, and what had gone wrong. I answered a couple of questions before entering Turf Moor for the final time. I watched the game from one of the boxes with several other players and was saddened when I heard the whistle blow to signal the end of the game. I enjoyed the company and the banter I had shared with my teammates at Burnley, and I knew the moment I walked out of the stadium, I'd probably never see most of them again. The fact that the team lost 1-0 didn't help the mood in the dressing room, but I said my goodbyes to the team and the physios before knocking on the manager's door and shaking hands with the coaching staff one last time.

21. Down but never out

I officially moved back to the United States in September of 2006 with an ambitious plan to rehabilitate my knee in time to join a Major League Soccer team at the start of the new season in 2007. I was in a difficult position. My experience at Burnley had left my confidence at rock-bottom, but that seemed to be the least of my worries. I couldn't shake the words that the doctor had told me back in England. *Maybe you should consider hanging up your boots.* Those simple yet powerful words were stuck in the back of my mind. I was flying back home with a plan, but that plan seemed distant and oddly out of my hands. My future was nothing more than a fuzzy cloud of uncertainty, an uncertainty that I wasn't particularly accustomed to. Though I was a bit unsure of my future after I left Arsenal, I knew I'd be playing the sport I loved come the start of the new season. My entire life I had been accustomed to setting many goals for myself, both long term and short term, that helped me get to where I wanted to be, but the doctor's words resonated, and I couldn't help but feel more unsure about things than ever before. What if it was really over? I was 22 years old and wasn't prepared to deal with it. Everything felt completely out of my control and that feeling haunted me.

Within a week of returning to Roanoke, I found myself on another plane, this time heading to Miami to pay a visit to Dr Uribe, the doctor who had performed my second knee surgery while I was still in high school. I wanted to clear my mind of everything and was planning on completing all my rehab in a sun-soaked Miami. Dr Uribe was wary of operating again. Every time a doctor entered the joint, I ran the risk of scarring, infection, and a host of other setbacks. He prescribed an aggressive rehab program, one that would help build the strength in my quads and hamstrings again. My leg had atrophied a bit from not being used, and Dr Uribe was hoping that strengthening the muscles around the joint would help support my knee better, thus alleviating the pain. I spent seven weeks in Miami before returning to Roanoke in October where I continued my exercises.

I could notice my muscles were getting bigger and stronger, but despite everything I'd done, my knee still just didn't feel right. I was struggling to go on a jog, walk long distances, or even stand for an extended period of time without feeling uncomfortable. Physically, I was back at home, living with my parents again. Mentally, a part of me was still at the Underhill Stadium replaying that stupid tackle that resulted in my most recent surgery. Another part could be found in Burnley, where I'd left my teammates and my most recent life. The rest of my mind was busy visiting the various MLS cities that might hold my future. People continuously asked me which team in MLS I'd be playing for the following year.

"If my knee gets better, hopefully…"

My default response was starting to wear me down. What if it didn't get better? Then what?

During my last few weeks in England I'd begun speaking with Craig Sharon, an agent out of Washington, D.C., whom I'd agreed to sign with if I was able to regain my health. He'd already contacted the League and was in the process of negotiating terms for a special lottery I'd be placed in as soon as I was cleared to play again. My fingers were crossed for D.C. United. It was the closest club to my hometown and I had some good friends who lived in and near the nation's capital. Craig arranged for me to see United's team doctor and also meet with their club's officials at a playoff game in October. My mood began improving. I was looking forward to the challenge of MLS and thrilled about getting the chance to play in front of my friends and family on a regular basis.

My parents and I made the three-and-a-half-hour drive up to Washington where we met with Dr Annunziata. As United's doctor he'd seen his fair share of sports-related injuries. His calm nature and warm personality gave me hope. By no means was he thrilled about the state of my knee, but he refused to completely write me off. One thing was certain, though. I'd require more surgery in order to make my knee playable again. After that, and depending on how my body dealt with the daily abuse of being a professional athlete, I might require more surgery again within two months or two years.

For the entire journey home my parents tried to convince me that what the doctor had said was positive. The possibility of playing again flickered in the horizon, behind the uncertainty of surgeries, an uncertainty that I'd become tired of. They knew what I wanted, but declared their support for whatever decision I wanted to make regardless.

The journey was a sobering one. I spent three and a half hours staring at the ceiling of my parents' Jeep wondering what the hell I was going to do. When we arrived home, I quietly went to my room, closed the door, and sat at my desk. My parents had left my room exactly the way it was in high school. Scarves of my favourite teams lined the walls while posters from various World Cups helped me relive some of football's finest moments on a daily basis. The 2003 edition of the U.S. National Team's annual poster hung adjacent to my bed. It hadn't been touched since I turned the page over three and a half years before. The month read "July", and a picture of Kasey Keller dominated the upper portion of the calendar. The only writing on the calendar was a phrase written in bold permanent marker on the fifth of July:

Move to London!

I made my way back downstairs and asked my parents to join me in the family room. My mom and dad both knew what was coming. Anna sat next to me and put her arm around me as I muttered my decision to stop playing to them. Everything had seemingly gone full circle. Sitting in the same room where I'd taken Steve Rowley's first phone call four and a half years before, my parents consoled me. My dad, quite possibly the most optimistic man ever, began convincing me that life without football was indeed possible.

I was finally able to call my best friends and answer the question that had been so frequently directed my way in the past months. Of course, everybody was sad about the decision I was being forced to make, but happy that I was no longer having it eat away at my sanity. To make sure that nobody was left out, I wrote a simple note on Facebook explaining my decision. The note was directed mostly towards my friends and family, but I also knew that some Arsenal, Ipswich Town, and Burnley fans that were part of my network would read it. I did not, however, know that my note would be copied and pasted into various forums, blogs, and websites by those fans.

The resulting kindness that erupted from my note was incredible. Thousands of messages flooded my inbox within the next couple of weeks, and I couldn't help but read each one. I was in a low place when I posted the note. Sure, I was relieved to know that the decision had been lifted off my shoulders, but that didn't mean I knew what I was going to do next, and it definitely didn't mean that whatever I chose would fill the void left by my inability to play football. The messages ranged from one sentence notes expressing sadness at my news to full blown paragraphs highlighting my best moments as a player. Nearly every note finished with one of three lines: *You'll always be a Gunner. You'll always be a Tractor Boy. You'll always be a Claret.* I still can't properly express how grateful I was to see all the messages.

Several days later I rang Steve Rowley and let him know about the decision I'd made. I soon received phone calls from Paul Irwin and other members of the staff at Arsenal expressing their best wishes for my future. Ipswich Town's chairman, David Sheepshanks, and their new manager and former captain during my stint at Town, Jim Magilton, both also sent letters to my house wishing me their best.

Despite all the kind words from everyone around me, all I wanted to do was dwell on everything that was happening. Did I feel bad for myself? Of course I did. Several months prior to my decision, I was running around and playing the sport that had made me happy as long as I could remember. I loved being a pro. Playing in front of crowds singing their hearts out for clubs with histories that spanned over a hundred years. I had so much more to prove, and my chances of fulfilling several of the dreams and goals I'd set for out for myself years before had seemingly been yanked right out from underneath me.

If moving to London and adapting to my new lifestyle there had been difficult, then motivating myself to get back on my feet and figure out exactly what I wanted to do with the rest of my life seemed nearly impossible. My interest in architecture had faded slightly since I was eighteen, and I wasn't really sure what exactly I was passionate about anymore. By February I had decided that I'd apply to Virginia Tech due to its proximity to Roanoke. Still, I had no idea what I wanted to study or what I wanted to be. Well I knew what I wanted to be. I wanted to be a footballer, but due to my circumstances that was no longer possible.

Several weeks before, Steve Rowley had called asking me if I had any plans to go into coaching. A potential partnership with the Colorado Rapids was on the horizon and both clubs were looking to get a coach involved at the youth level. I expressed a bit of interest but had never coached in my life and wasn't really sure I was ready to move to Denver so soon after making my decision to end my playing career. Mentally I was still in an incredibly fragile state. I was happy having my family and friends nearby and wasn't ecstatic at the prospect of moving several thousand miles away. Steve told me that he'd get back to me as soon as he was given more details.

Sometime in March Steve called back. In a couple of days I was set to have a meeting with admissions at Virginia Tech and figure out exactly what my plan for school would be. I hadn't really thought much about the coaching gig since Steve's initial call, so when he told me that the coaching position we'd discussed required years of experience I wasn't really upset about it.

"Both the Rapids and Arsenal are looking to get a more experienced guy out in Colorado," he said. "Even though the coaching option is out, several of us, including the Boss, were wondering what you'd think about being our North American Scout."

Well those words certainly managed to catch me off guard.

"A scout? Like you?" I couldn't have tripped over my words any more if I'd tried.

"Well, yea. You'd be working for me and covering the States, Mexico, and Canada. I want you think about it hard, Danny. Don't make any quick decisions and speak to your parents about it. I know school is important for you, and I don't want you to regret anything."

Once again a phone call from Steve Rowley had forged a massive fork in the middle of the road. He'd told me to think hard about it and not make a hasty decision, but I knew what I wanted to do the moment he'd asked. The thought of travelling throughout North America looking for Arsenal's future stars excited me. I wouldn't be able to live out some of the soccer dreams I'd set out for myself anymore, but what if I could help others live out theirs?

The call from Steve had certainly come out of nowhere, and within a couple of weeks I was back in London for my two-week, full-blown scouting education. Like many people throughout the world, I was confident that I could recognise a talented player if I saw one. The two weeks in London opened my eyes and gave me the unique experience of sitting next to some of the best scouts in the world during games. Nearly every day that I was there I'd go out with one of the English-based scouts and watch a game – some of them were first team games while others were youth matches. Each game provided me with an opportunity to assess a player we were following and report back to Steve on him. Steve would grade my report, making very clear the information he wanted to see when I wrote about interesting players.

As a scout I had to learn how to watch a game from a different angle. Coaches enjoy watching games and making points about how a team's shape affects the play, what a team's weaknesses and strengths are, and so on. When watching games with coaches I find myself talking a lot about what could have been done differently as a team to get the desired result. During my scouting training I was asked to watch a specific player and report on him. It was difficult for me to get used to watching a single player out of twenty-two for ninety minutes, but I soon became accustomed to it. During this time I began to realise just how difficult it is for a player to impress a scout enough for recommendation. The players we look at need to excel in a variety of categories, but it almost always comes down to intelligence and technique.

I found it very interesting conversing with Steve and the other scouts about intelligence. As a player I knew football intelligence was important on the pitch but never realised just how important it was. Most things can be improved, but a player's intelligence seems to either be there or not be there. Everything, from the weight of a pass to which foot a pass is played to, can be filed under intelligence. If a teammate has a defender on his left shoulder then the guy with the ball has to play the ball to his right foot. The environment in a game is constantly changing, and it's the most intelligent of players who are able to adapt and thrive.

It was no fluke that Cesc made his debut at the age of 16 for Arsenal. The Boss was confident enough in his technical ability as well as his intelligence to start him as a central midfielder against Rotherham in the Carling Cup in 2003. For a kid who would have been in the middle of his sophomore year in high school had he grown up in the States, Cesc controlled the midfield against a team of seasoned professionals that night at Highbury. His awareness was superb and has only improved since he playfully sprayed balls around Rotherham's defenders. I didn't know then, but his intelligence levels on the pitch would have made any top scout drool. The little things he did and continues to do at the top level make him very difficult to defend. He's constantly checking his shoulders, making sure he is aware of his opponents' positions, his teammates' positions, and his own position on the pitch. Before the ball gets to him, he knows where the ball needs to go. Of course, not every player in the world is Cesc, but intelligence plays a vital part for any player at the top level.

Equal in importance with intelligence comes technique. This was an easy concept for me to grasp because of my time at the club as a player. I knew the technical skill a player needed to possess was extremely high because I'd seen so many players come and go from the club due to their lack of technique. Once again, the free flowing, sharp, and efficient style of Arsenal's game is no fluke. We look for players who are able to remain composed and keep the ball moving no matter how fast a game gets. The first team during my time at the club contained some of the most technically gifted players the world has ever seen. Dennis Bergkamp's first touch was incredible. Robert Pires' ability to side foot a ball from twenty yards out into the side-netting of the goal, just out of the grasp of a fully-stretched goalkeeper, was equally impressive. I remember playing against Everton at Highbury and knowing that no matter what, I could always give the ball to Edu and he'd control the ball and keep it moving. With pressure on his back and both sides, Edu would still demand the ball and manage to retain possession. We don't look for the guys who panic when the first sign of defensive pressure is evident. We look for the guys who are technically superior, confident in that technique, and composed enough to keep the ball when two, three, and even four guys are around them.

Another extremely important aspect of any player I report on is their work ethic and attitude. This is probably the most simple but overlooked quality for young players. If you lose the ball, get it back. The top level has no time for players who think they are exempt from defending just because they are listed as attacking players. Every player has a duty defensively as well as offensively. If a player thinks he is above working hard for his team, then he will quickly fall out of favour with his teammates and, more importantly, the coaching staff. The English Premier League is a tough league, and no matter what team a scout works for, I can guarantee you he is looking for a player who is always willing to leave everything he has out on the pitch after ninety minutes. Players need to be fit and tough, both mentally and physically.

Walking through those same glass double doors that I'd walked through as a seventeen-year-old trialist for the first time felt so good again. I was happy to be back at the club that had given me an opportunity to make a name for myself in the world of football. The staff had remained mostly the same, and the first team had changed slightly – of course, the departure of Patrick Vieira was probably the biggest difference in the squad.

Amongst the first teamers and playing far more regularly than they had been when I was still living in England, were Cesc, Gael Clichy, and Philippe Senderos. I'd only been out of London for two years but the progress my three friends had made was incredible. This is what made football such an incredible industry to be involved in. The three of them by 2007 had collectively played in a Champions League Final, the Premier League, and the World Cup. Philippe had actually even scored for Switzerland in the World Cup in Germany. Memories of Carling Cup and reserve team games with the three of them were still fresh in my mind, but my former teammates had developed the way they'd been expected to and were now household names throughout London, England, and the world of football.

Their star-power was both strange and extremely interesting for me to experience. Only a couple of years previously I'd ridden the tube with both Cesc and Phil into Central London and nobody had remotely recognised either of them. Now they couldn't walk to their local grocery store without being recognised, asked for an autograph, or heckled by a supporter of a rival team.

During my first trip back to London as a scout Phil and I walked into a Tesco Express to pick up some milk and yogurt when a Tottenham supporter recognised him. As mentioned, Phil had already played in a World Cup and had helped Arsenal get to the final of the Champions League in 2006. I'm not sure why I was so surprised at the Tottenham fan's reaction when he saw Phil, because I knew how deep the rivalries ran in England, especially between Arsenal and Spurs. I couldn't help but be amazed, however. The guy literally just followed us around, telling Phil he was garbage while singing Spurs' songs. His drunken stupor and slurred words were comical, to say the least, but it did seem to get quite hostile after a couple of minutes, especially since Phil didn't acknowledge him. Several Arsenal fans just happened to walk in a couple of minutes after it all started and eventually intervened before asking Phil for autographs. Both sides of the fan spectrum had been put on display that night - the hatred and disdain for an opposing club's player by one fan, and the support, love, and loyalty for that same player by fans of our club. In short, it was cool. Most importantly, however, my friends, with all this newfound fame and adoration, had been able to maintain level heads.

Sticking with the same theme, another funny situation presented itself to Cesc and me the night of a Cup fixture against Spurs in the winter of 2008. The Boss had made the decision to rest Cesc. He'd played in a large number of games in the previous weeks and needed a break. That morning Cesc had asked me if I wanted to come to his flat after training and then go to the Emirates together in his car. Arsenal fans that have been to the Emirates know just how difficult it is to navigate around the stadium in a car. The streets are flooded with people pouring out of pubs, restaurants, the tube, and even work. The closest roads to the stadium are closed off to traffic almost an hour before kick-off because of all the pedestrian traffic.

Cesc had never been left out of the squad since the club had moved to the Emirates, and he wasn't entirely sure how he was meant to get to the players' car park with police roadblocks and fans everywhere. We slowly crept along the perimeter the police had set up around the stadium, asking each set of cops if we could get by to get into the stadium. Despite our best efforts Cesc's Spanish accent and shiny black Mercedes weren't enough to gain us entry. All I could do was laugh. *Man you really are famous! Can't even get into your own stadium!*

Our situation, though comical and irritating all at once, soon became desperate. We'd circled the stadium twice with no luck and were beginning to get slightly nervous.

While waiting for a light to change at an intersection, I told Cesc I had an idea and got out of the car. Parked in front of us was a typical Metropolitan Police riot van filled to the brim with cops in riot gear. A metal grate was pulled down over the windshield to protect it from thrown objects, and the stares I received from each heavily-clad, shield-wielding policeman inside were slightly concerning.

I managed to convince the driver to roll his window down, and the look he fired my way was especially disturbing.

"Hi. Umm. Yea, my buddy and I are having a bit of trouble getting into the stadium because all the roads are closed. I understand how this shouldn't be an issue, but its Cesc."

The policeman stared at me for a couple of seconds, probably wondering why some American kid was standing two feet from him, blabbering about wanting to get into the stadium, on a match day, when Spurs were visiting.

Just as he was about to speak, I heard the voice of one of the policemen in the back of the riot van.

"I'm pretty sure he's telling the truth. Car's got Spanish plates and it looks just like him."

Another fully armoured policeman in the back agreed and told the driver it was indeed Cesc.

The driver turned back to me, smiled, and said two words: "Follow us."

Just as he finished his statement, the lights and sound of the van's siren erupted into the night. I hurried back to Cesc's car and passed along the driver's message. The sea of traffic parted, and within three minutes we were at the entrance to the players' underground car park. The driver, a huge smirk across his face, shouted "This close enough!?" before driving off. Paul Irwin, who had been at the main entrance as our police escort pulled us in, couldn't stop laughing at the desperate measures we'd taken to make sure were on time. He did manage to gather himself for long enough to call us "Big Time Charlies" as we walked by. Things had definitely changed for my friends.

The fame that accompanies the players isn't always a positive, however, and I noticed that simple day-to-day affairs had become very different for my friends. After training one day during my first trip back as a scout, Cesc and I headed into Enfield to grab something at HMV, a DVD and game store popular throughout England. Cesc parked on the street and said he'd be right back. Ten minutes later I saw Cesc running out of HMV with a hoard of children behind him. He got back in the car laughing and said that the store owner had kicked him out for creating such a disturbance in the shop when all he really wanted to do was get a new Xbox game that had come out. He wasn't able to buy the game, and, to top things off, the attention that he had drawn in the store attracted a car full of angry Tottenham fans who decided they were going to stop their car in front of us at the traffic lights and not let us go when the light turned green. They literally just sat at the light, calling us all sorts of expletives while making very disturbing faces. We laughed at first, but then realised they weren't moving. Whenever Cesc tried to make a move around them, they would move their car and block us in. Finally, one of the guys opened the door and Cesc pulled a manoeuvre worthy of a Hollywood action flick to get us out of the busy town and back to relative safety.

It would be a lie if I said that I wasn't envious of what my friends had come to achieve, but it's all good natured and I wish them nothing but success and health in their careers. As for me, prior to the phone call that had brought me back into the English football world, I had shied away from the sport I loved and couldn't stand to watch games on television or in person knowing that I couldn't even jog ten yards without my knee hurting. It was like a bad break up with a girl, and I thought that if I quit football cold turkey, I'd be able to move on and hopefully be able to rekindle some sort of friendship with the sport in the distant future. Mentally it was tough for me to watch, because when I was growing up I always used to practise after watching games. To watch a game and just sit on my butt once it ended was unnatural, and I figured the only thing I could do to prevent getting upset was not watch football at all.

My philosophy has changed since being hired as a scout in March of 2007, and although it's still sometimes difficult to sit and watch kids grace the same fields I used to when I was growing up, it is starting to become easier for me. My dream as a kid growing up in Roanoke was to sign professional forms with a big European club and play in front of deafening crowds in sold-out stadiums. My dream as an eighteen-year-old living in London remained unchanged, and I did everything I could to reach my goals and continually live out my dream. Unfortunately, my injuries prevented me from every really establishing myself at the top level, and I have been forced to reconsider everything I have ever aspired to do. I never got the chance to fulfil my dream of playing in a World Cup, and although I like to believe that no dream is wasted, the likelihood of me ever playing football again, let alone in a World Cup, is very slim. The thing about life that is very interesting, however, is the fact that it goes on, and curveballs are thrown when they are least expected.

I'm a firm believer in setting goals and dreams for yourself to work towards. I love waking up every morning and going to bed every night thinking of ways to better reach my goals and targets. My advice to anyone wanting to become a professional football player, a world-renowned lawyer, a top trader on Wall Street, a college student, or anything in between is to dream big. A dream is something that you think about and yearn for and hope you will someday obtain. The more you think about your dream, the more you will do to achieve it. Nothing ever comes without hard work and dedication, however, and if becoming a professional football player is really what you dream of becoming, then working hard on your own and with your team should become second nature to you. If you ever think you have become good enough and deserve to be given a chance, you will become your own biggest enemy. Even the best professionals in the world are constantly looking for ways to improve. No player is ever complete, and the learning process continues even when players are winding down their careers in their mid-thirties.

The players who are given a shot at their dreams are the players who perform even when they think no one is watching. Players should play every game as if it's their last, because with life and sports, you never know when you may be putting your boots on for the final time. This is the mentality that is required to make it at the top level. Only a small percentage of players are good enough to be considered irreplaceable, and even those players aren't really guaranteed anything. If it's your dream to succeed on the world stage, then know that you share the same dream as millions of other kids from around the world, kids who may not be lucky enough to afford two hundred dollar boots and the best ball on the market, kids who don't know where their next meal is coming from and play football barefoot on dirt fields using a ball made of string. If you are lucky enough and good enough to be spotted and do end up signing a professional contract at sixteen, seventeen, or eighteen, please realise that the work has just begun and you have a long way to go before you can even think about taking your foot off the pedal. Take the opportunity by the scruff of the neck and do everything you can to be the best you can be, while keeping your dreams and the big picture in check. The very least you can ever do is fight as hard as you can and try your hardest. If you don't succeed, make sure it is because of your ability and not because of your lack of effort. If things don't go as planned and life takes an unexpected turn, then be prepared to adjust and create new dreams if necessary.

I once heard a quote on a television show that went as follows, "I look up to the people that can carve a life for themselves once their dreams have died." Unfortunately for me, my dreams of playing in a World Cup and the Premiership and Champions League died when my knee decided to call it quits. I was 22 years old when I retired and quickly realised that my life was only just beginning and I'd have to focus my energy on new dreams and goals if I was going to make it in this world. My new job as a scout has brought with it new responsibilities, adventures, and targets I'd like to reach. My goals have shifted from scoring in big time matches to finding players who can score in big time matches for Arsenal - finding players who can get into Arsenal's first team and make a difference. These goals won't be easy to attain, and I may never attain them, but they are the goals that fuel my dreams, and I'll do everything in my power to someday reach them.

In terms of my general health, I underwent big surgery in February of 2008 to hopefully fix my knee problem once and for all. Several weeks before my operating date, Arsenal America held a dinner in my honour, officially making me the fan club's Honorary President. The celebration took place in an intimate banquet room at one of

Washington, D.C.'s fantastic restaurants. Members of the fan club, as well as my mom and a small group of my friends, were all invited to dinner where I was presented with a wonderful trophy commemorating the night. Once dinner had ended, I answered an array of questions from the fans and took pictures before calling it a night. I was and still am incredibly honoured to be a part of Arsenal America, and it made me feel a lot better about my situation in general before my big date with the surgeon.

I was told that my February 19th operation would be the largest of all the surgeries I'd faced and that after a three-hour procedure, I'd have a new transplanted meniscus, as well as four screws and a metal plate on my tibia. My surgery was completed in Chicago where I spent four weeks taking twenty-six pills a day for pain and inflammation. I then flew to Los Angeles and specifically *Athletes' Performance* to start my rehab. I spent three months in Los Angeles with one of the best therapists in the country before flying back to Richmond, Virginia to resume life and continue rehab. I went from using two crutches to using one crutch, and then graduated to a cane for several months. A year later, as I write this in March of 2009, I am still recovering and jogged my first ten yards in two years several weeks ago. I'm still a long way from a complete recovery, but I'm treating my rehab with the same fight and determination that I treated my soccer career. I may be able to kick around a little once this is all said and done, but most importantly I want to be comfortable in my daily activities. I've become a cycling enthusiast and hope to one day compete in a big race with the world's best. Sure it's lofty, but it's a dream, and if a boy from the Blue Ridge Mountains in Roanoke, Virginia can pull an Arsenal shirt over his head and score a match-winner in injury time for the club he's come to love, then what's preventing him from doing anything else he wants to do?

My love for football developed as soon as I was able to walk and has blossomed into a lasting romance that has brought me to tears for both good and bad reasons. The fact that football is so global makes it unique in the world of sports. I visited Europe to play football for the first time when I was fourteen and somehow managed to fall even deeper in love with the sport than I had been before. I've been to over twenty countries because of the beautiful game, and every experience has been a lesson that no book in the world could ever teach.

I always knew I'd become a professional football player, but I never knew how it would happen or when it would happen. I always knew, because I spent more time dreaming about the sport than about anything else. Every day of my life growing up, I'd dream – I'd dream of getting the chance to walk out of a tunnel in front of thousands of die-hard fans screaming their aching lungs out, splashing every ounce of their emotion into the atmosphere for all to hear. I dreamed of being one of the world's best players and being idolised by every young aspiring player in the world. I dreamed of scoring game-winning goals and celebrating in front of millions on television. I dreamed. Through the combination of an unbelievable amount of hard work, practice, timing, a bit of luck, and fate, my dreams were turned into a reality. Henry David Thoreau once said, "Do not worry if you have built your castles in the air. They are where they should be. Now put the foundations under them." I urge everyone to dream as wildly as you possibly can, work until you can't possibly work anymore and fall over, get up and work a little more, smile throughout the journey, and enjoy the wonderful ride it will take you on. Anything is possible, and I am more than happy to attest to that.

Epilogue

When I set out to write this book in 2008, I didn't particularly have a plan. I'd just had the surgery that would effectively end any chance I'd ever have of playing football again, and mentally I was a bit of a wreck. I was always used to having surgery, then getting back to a rigorous therapy programme that would ultimately get me back on the pitch in several weeks or months. There would be no return to the pitch, though. No return to my teammates. No return to the game that had given me so much.

Instead, after surgery I had my family and friends. My family in Chicago opened their home to my mom and me and went above and beyond anything I could ever imagine when it came to looking after us. What I'm most grateful for, though, is their eagerness to ask about my time in England that led me to write this book. My uncle came into my room one morning before work and said, "I want to hear about your goal against City when I come back from work tonight."

That day I pulled out my laptop and began writing about the goal. First, the actual play and Cesc's pass, then the post-match celebrations. Then I wrote about the pre-match experience. When my uncle returned, he read it, and then asked, "What happened next?" I began expanding on the story, jotting down stories and things I remembered about training, games, and life in general.

Years later I finally have a story that I'm happy to remember about my playing days and the beginning of my time as a scout. Though that portion of my life has been wrapped up and will never change, so much has happened since then and I still have so much I aim to do in my life.

In the summer of 2010, I received an email from Alex Yi, a friend of mine who had played in the US Youth National Teams and had gone pro himself. He was now helping coach a team in the DC area and wanted to introduce me to Matt Pilkington, the head coach of the team he was helping out. Matt sent me an email explaining that he had an interesting kid in his team who had a German passport. At the time, the boy was 13, but despite being so young, his German passport made him very enticing. My schedule at the time was quite busy, but I kept in touch with Matt and eventually planned a trip to see his U15 team train outside Washington, D.C. in January of 2011.

I'll never forget the night for two reasons: 1) January in DC is cold, and the night I chose to sit on the metal benches adjacent to the pitch on which Gedion Zelalem was training was no exception; 2) I needed just 10 minutes to realise how much potential Gedion had. Of course, I knew he'd have loads of work to do if he was ever to make it in the world of football, but I liked what I saw. Technically he was excellent and his awareness on and off the ball was unlike anything I'd seen in my region up to that point. I left the session that night excited to follow up and eager to see Gedion play again soon.

At the time, I was living in Richmond, Virginia, so the two-hour drive to Bethesda, Maryland was an easy one. I watched Gedion play in three or four league games and one more training session before deciding I wanted to bring him in on trial. Through the help of the Richmond Strikers, a team Arsenal was partnered with at the time, we also brought him down to Richmond to guest play in a tournament so Steve Morrow, former Arsenal player and current head of recruitment in the Academy, could also take a look. We both agreed he was worth having over to London and the planning began.

Because of his age and the rules put in place for transfers, we had to wait several years before we could do anything with Gedion, which was quite stressful for everyone. During that time, I got to know Gedion's family quite well and ensured that both his family and the club were aware of what was going on and when he'd be over next.

When he was finally old enough to move over full-time, Gedion traded the United States capital for England's capital. Though the process was quite long from start to finish, he became the first player I scouted who would eventually go on to sign for Arsenal.

After a slow first four years as a scout in CONCACAF, my break had finally come. Little did I know it but another player was going to catch my eye shortly after I first saw Gedion.

My next player came in the form of a Costa Rican I first saw in Guatemala in 2011. Joel Campbell and his Costa Rican side were looking to qualify for the U20 World Cup, and I'd been tipped off that he was quite an interesting talent. Though I'd seen some exciting players during my first several years as a scout, including Javier Hernandez who would eventually go on to sign for Manchester United, Joel was the first senior level player who really seemed to make an impact on me. He was fast, strong, hard-working, and had a confidence about him that I quite liked.

In Guatemala, I watched him score six goals and knew I'd continue tracking him throughout the summer. He was called into Costa Rica's full national team for the Gold Cup as well as Copa America, which proved to be perfect for me. At the U20 level, he was good, but I was eager to see how he'd do against older, stronger, better competition. The Gold Cup and Copa America would provide that platform for him to prove to me that he was worth going in for. On top of that, he had the U20 World Cup in Colombia to look forward to as well. Needless to say, it was a busy summer for Joel as well as me.

During the Gold Cup that year, I flew from city to city, day after day following Joel, the US National Team, and Mexico's National Team. His performances solidified my interest in him, and the reports I continued to send to Steve Rowley expressed my desire to take the next steps with him. Another South American scout of ours watched him during Copa America confirming my observations before we finally moved in to make the deal happen. Other clubs had entered the mix at that point, but we won the race for his signature and, in the process, I'd finally signed my first player. (Gedion was still too young to move over, so I was still driving up and down from DC to see him and his family every other week. Despite seeing Gedion first, Joel became the first player I signed because of how quickly we were able to get the deal done.) Several days later the Boss called to congratulate me. For whatever reason his number came up as unknown on my phone, and though I nearly declined the call, I answered to hear his voice on the other end.

The process of identifying, backing, and eventually signing Joel was what I'd signed up for in the first place. I was ecstatic finally to get my first player, even if I hadn't even met him! My goal as a scout was to find a player of interest to the Boss, Steve, and the club. I'd managed to do it and couldn't wait to have Gedion's situation sorted and finalised as well.

Since then, it's been amazing to see the progress both Gedion and Joel have made in their careers. Both have represented Arsenal in the Champions League and made various first team appearances during their time at the club. Joel starred for Costa Rica in the 2014 World Cup in Brazil while Gedion has committed his future to the US National Team and has represented the States at the U20 and U23 levels. Of course, both players would likely have been seen and scouted eventually, but it always gives me great joy when I see them playing on television, especially in Arsenal shirts.

I spent a few more years full time with Arsenal after Joel and Gedion signed with the club. On top of my scouting I also worked alongside Steve Morrow in an initiative he led to promote the Arsenal way strategically around the world. Our goal was simple: develop and identify players globally who could one day make the transition to London and represent the club. I've since scaled back my travelling, scouting, and coaching, but continue to help Arsenal in their scouting efforts.

Since then I've also focused heavily on a new project I started several years ago with a good friend of mine. In an effort to leverage some of the great relationships we've developed over the years with some of the world's best players, agents, and clubs around the world, we started SWOL - or Soccer Without Limits - and are now focused on Fury 90, a mobile fantasy manager game designed to engage football fans globally and bring them closer to their favourite stars and clubs. Though building something from the ground up is never easy, I've enjoyed the challenges we've had to overcome and look forward to growing the company into something special for both the fans as well as professional players and clubs worldwide.

Football has given me so much. As a kid watching my dad at the weekend, I always knew it was something I wanted to do. The sport has opened door after door and presented me with more opportunities than I could have ever imagined. Of course, things may not have worked out the way I'd wanted them to from a playing standpoint, but I have no regrets and will always look back fondly on my time as a young kid trying to navigate my way through England's incredible football world. Even flipping through the pages of this book and remembering the mindset I had as a boy with a mountain to climb puts a smile on my face. Though I'll never be able to do some of the things I'd set out to do in my youth, I still use that belief and confidence across all facets of life. To me, no dream is ever too big or too small, and I look forward to applying that to whatever challenges are thrown my way in the future.

1. WITH STEVE ROWLEY

2. RESERVES LONDON COLNEY

3. SECOND YEAR AT ARSENAL

4. SCORING AT MANCHESTER CITY

5. CELEBRATING WITH SEBASTIAN LARSSEN

6. CELEBRATING WITH PHILIPPE SENDEROS AND JOHAN DJOUROU

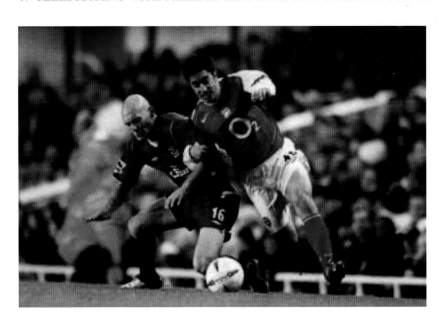

7. FACING THOMAS GRAVESON. ARSENAL V EVERTON AT HIGHBURY

8. TRACTOR BOY: PLYMOUTH V IPSWICH

9. A SCOUT FOR ARSENAL

Photos

Front cover photos

- Time to celebrate in front of the travelling fans – Robin van Persie, me, Johan Djourou, Sebastian Larsson, Cesc Fabregas, Justin Hoyte, and Quincy Owusu-Abeyie all take in the moment.
- With Arsène Wenger and Gedion Zelalem at the training ground after Gedion's trial.

Page 161-164

1. Steve Rowley and me watching first team training.
2. Finding my feet during my first year in a reserve team game held behind closed doors at London Colney.
3. Stronger, more confident and full of belief – the start of my second year at Arsenal, trying to make it as a left-back.
4. My debut at Manchester City and the goal – I'd grown up watching Danny Mills play on television for club and country. Now it was my turn
5. A special night for Seb and me – we'd become close friends, and getting to make our debuts and share a moment of celebration like this after the goal was special.
6. Philippe Senderos and Johan Djourou, my two giant Swiss friends, celebrate with me after the final whistle. They both made their debuts that night as well
7. Strength – Thomas Graveson was one of the strongest players I ever faced. Here against Everton at Highbury
8. On the road for Ipswich at Plymouth during the busy holiday period. My first start for the Tractor Boys.
9. Back in London. New job, new stadium, same crest.

Glossary

One of the biggest advantages of moving to England as opposed to another country to play football was the fact that I didn't have to learn a new language. Being able to speak and understand the language in any new country is a massive boost, and I was glad that I didn't have to worry about that side of my adjustment. However it only took a few weeks for me to realise that the English that was being spoken in England sounded a lot different from the English I was used to hearing and speaking on a daily basis.

Below is a list of words that I frequently heard and started using during my stay in the United Kingdom. There are hundreds of other words and phrases that didn't make the list, but I heard these the most and selected only a choice few.

- Bangers and Mash – A typical dish in England consisting of sausages (bangers) and mashed potatoes (mash).
- Biscuits – cookies
- Bloke/Geezer – another word for "man"
- Bollocks/The Dog's bollocks - the word bollocks actually means "testicles" but isn't used that way very often. When used alone, bollocks generally means "crap" i.e. "That's bollocks!" However, when used as "the dog's bollocks", its used to describe how great something is, ie., "John's new car is the dog's bollocks!".
- Bonnet – the hood of a car.
- Boot – the trunk of a car.
- Boots - cleats
- Bus/Coach – when talking about modes of transport, the English seem quite particular in distinguishing the difference between the mode of public transportation and the likes of a Greyhound bus. City busses are still called busses, but the team busses that players ride on to games are known as coaches.
- Butty – a Northern term used to describe a sandwich. Usually has butter spread on the it.
- Car hire – car rental. The word "hire" generally means "rent".
- Chav – a derogative term used to describe a person who is generally from the lower class and uneducated. Chavs usually wear sportswear with tacky jewellery with the desire to show off a wealth that doesn't exist with knock-off designer labels.
- Cheeky – used to describe someone who is unmannerly, impertinent, and possibly inappropriate. Often used as "cheeky chappy" or "cheeky monkey".

166

- Chip Shop/Chippy – a take away restaurant that serves fish and chips.
- Chips – French fries
- Cockney Rhyming Slang – one of the most fascinating and mind-boggling characteristics of the United Kingdom that never ceases to amaze me and make me laugh. Even though it originated and is widely used in East London, some of the more popular phrases are nationally used. Words and phrases are formed by rhyming a word or series of words with the intended subject. For instance, when referring to the stairs, people will say "apples and pears." It can get even more confusing when certain words are dropped and assumed. For example, when referring to someone's hair, people will simply say "Barnet", which comes from "Barnet Fair." When listening to two Cockney's who use rhyming slang liberally speak, it is very confusing and sounds like the two people are talking about absolutely nothing in particular. In fact, when you hear someone say something like, "I fell down the apples and pears (stairs), cut my boat race (face), and now have this mars bar (scar)," it sounds as if they really need help! Several of my teammates at Ipswich Town referred to me simply as "septic", which 'obviously' means 'yank' (septic tank = yank).
- Crisps – potato chips
- Custard Pie –obviously a dessert, but also used to describe a situation where someone is completely ignored or looked over. If a guy were to be shut down by a girl after he approached her and asked for her number, the guy's friends might say, "You got pied."
- Dodgy – comparable to the word "sketchy" in the United States
- Dual Carriageway – two lane road
- En suite – usually meaning a bathroom that is in a bedroom, like the master bedroom
- Fag – a cigarette
- Fiver/Tenner/Score – a five pound note, a ten pound note, and a twenty pound note (currency)
- Flat – apartment
- Footie – soccer
- Gaff – often used to refer to someone's house. "I'm at my gaff", but also used in the phrase "all over the gaff", which means "all over the place". For example, "John's been all over the gaff recently because of his new travelling sales job."
- Gaffer/The Boss – terms of respect used to address and refer to the manager (coach) of a sports team.

- Garage – gas station, car mechanic, or place to park your car. Rhymes with "carriage".
- Holiday – vacation
- Jammy – lucky. "He's so jammy."
- Lemonade – a carbonated soft drink that probably has 0% fruit juice and doesn't remotely compare to the lemonade Americans are used to drinking.
- Mullered – can be used to describe several things. 1) When someone is beaten up quite badly, they are said to have been mullered. 2) In sports, when a team comprehensively beats another team. "Arsenal mullered Chelsea 7-0 in the League." 3) When someone drinks so much they are basically belligerent and uncontrollable. "After 10 pints at the pub, they were all mullered and needed to be taken home."
- Mobile – cell phone
- Motorway – highway
- Nando's – Portuguese chain chicken restaurant that is quite possibly the best fast-food place I have ever enjoyed. Very popular amongst footballers. I visited Nando's at least twice a week if not more with Moritz, Seb, and Ingi. Get the Perinaise dip with your 'chips'.
- Oi – comparable to "Hey!" An exclamation to gain attention or show excitement. If someone is megged in a small sided game, players might yell out "Oi! Oi!" in excitement and appreciation.
- The Old Bill – the Police
- Pants – underwear
- Paracetamol – pain relief medication similar to Tylenol.
- Pear-shaped – when something goes wrong. "It all went pear-shaped."
- Petrol – gasoline
- Quid – slang for pounds (currency). Similar to the word "bucks" in the United States
- The rezzy's – term used to describe the reserve team. "He's playing in the rezzy's tonight."
- Row Z – pronounced "Row Zed" and referring to the highest row of seats in the stadium. When someone says, "He put it in Row Z", it's referring to someone kicking the ball as high and far away as possible, like a clearance.
- Rubbish/Bin – can be used to say trash/trashcan or when describing something that is worthless or useless. "The new CD I bought yesterday is rubbish."
- Sir - growing up in the States, I was taught from an early age to address my elders using 'sir' and 'ma'am'. In the United Kingdom, the use of the word 'sir' is restricted to those men who have been knighted by the Queen of

England. Most of the people that I called 'sir' would laugh and tell me they hadn't been knighted…yet.

- Skint – broke, out of money.
- Sound – basically means 'alright'. For example, "He's sound mate, thanks."
- Stone – a measurement for weight that is roughly fourteen pounds. Players in the UK usually refer to their weight in terms of stones or kilograms.
- Telly – television, as opposed to telephone.
- Tesco – probably my favourite grocery store in England, with some being far bigger than others. Tesco always made me laugh because some had signs saying "Open 24 hours" with a list of hours under the sign that had them open until 10 or 11pm. Maybe they meant open 24 hours a week.
- Top Drawer - a phrase used by people all over the country referring to something that is really good. If a player scored a really nice goal, someone might say, "His goal was top drawer." It almost sounds as if they are saying, "top draw."
- Track suit – what most athletes in the United States refer to as a warm-up suit.
- Trainers – running shoes/sneakers
- Trousers – pants
- Tube/Underground – London's subway system. Intimidating at first, but unbelievably easy to use after you get the hang of it.
- WC/Loo – the loo and the water closet are interchangeable and simply mean bathroom
- Yob – a young troublemaker. Whenever young kids made the newspaper headlines for the wrong reasons, the headlines would always read, "Woman Attacked by Yobs." I had no idea what a yob was in my first couple of months and imagined it to be some sort of animal or something. Yob is boy spelled backwards.

Acknowledgements

First and foremost I want to thank my family for being the most supportive, loving, and understanding family ever – I love you; my better half, Cortney, who brings the best out of me every day and continues to support me and my passions regardless of how silly they may seem sometimes; Imad Tsay, for convincing me to turn such a lofty and far-fetched idea into a wonderful reality; both sets of relatives in Chicago and Los Angeles for treating my mom and me like royalty after my big surgery; Danny Beamer and the Roanoke Star for providing me with a club and a base for me to grow up and thrive in; the small group of friends that I would constantly harass with drafts of my chapters to see if they were at all interesting and worth reading; the rest of my friends who have always been there for me regardless of my success with soccer; all the fans from Arsenal Football Club, Burnley Football Club, and Ipswich Town Football Club who, in both my brightest and darkest moments, showed me what fans are for – I will forever be grateful; and Steve Rowley, for giving me the chance to change my life and fulfil my wildest dreams with one simple phone call.